QUICK SIMPLE FOOD

QUICK SIMPLE FOOD

SUSIE QUICK

PHOTOGRAPHS BY LISA RUTLEDGE

CLARKSON POTTER / PUBLISHERS

NEW YORK

Copyright © 2003 by Susie Quick
Photographs copyright © 2003 by Lisa Rutledge
Styling by Susie Quick

Published by Clarkson Potter/Publishers,
New York, New York.
Member of the Crown Publishing Group,
a division of Random House, Inc.
www.randomhouse.com

CLARKSON N. POTTER is a trademark and
POTTER and colophon are registered trademarks
of Random House, Inc.

Printed in China

Design by Caitlin Daniels Israel

Library of Congress Cataloging-in-Publication Data

Quick, Susan, 1959–
Quick simple food / Susie Quick ; photographs by Lisa Rutledge.
p. cm.
1. Quick and easy cookery. 2. Cookery (Natural foods) I. Title.
TX833.5 .Q56/ 641.5'55—dc21   2002151387

ISBN 0-609-61071-6

10 9 8 7 6 5 4 3 2 1

First Edition

Contents

Introduction   1

Salads   16

Vegetables   44

Noodles, Rice, Grains   64

Soups and Stews   92

Meat, Chicken, Fish   120

Desserts   164

Acknowledgments   194

Index   195

Introduction

I learned to cook in my mother's kitchen, which meant I knew the importance of cooking food a long time for safety's sake, and that a little bacon grease never hurt anybody. Preparing dinner took up the better part of the afternoon once you figured in peeling potatoes, washing armfuls of fresh greens, and making hot rolls, iced tea, and dessert (cake or pie, never purchased), on top of whatever had been roasting in the oven since noon. Mom's cooking was delicious, but it was work. (Naps were not uncommon afterward.)

When I first got married I'd go home from a full day of work as a newspaper reporter and prepare what I thought was a proper dinner. By this time I had moved way beyond Mom's homespun repertoire to the food magazines. *Bon Appétit* was my beacon, *Cuisine* my constant companion. I made my own baguettes, stuffed a duck with figs, and composed a chilled seafood terrine layered with the colors of the Italian flag. I served "courses" on weeknights, for God's sake. Good thing my late-working husband arrived home around nine o'clock. One night as I placed his plate before him, he looked up at me and asked, "Soufflé . . . *again?*" I cooked this way for years because deep down I believed that food could be delicious only through hours of slavish effort.

But as my life got busier (and I shed my high-maintenance husband), my cooking style evolved. And so did what and how I ate. I learned how to cook simply and with a

sense of discovery and enjoyment. The fact that the foods I loved happened to be as good for me as they were delicious was an added blessing. I know a lot of people today have similar issues: They live their lives at a brisk walk—if not a steady jog—and making a home-cooked meal the same way their grandmother did just doesn't fit into the program. Also, the idea of heating up something ironically called a "meal solution" (or a faux "speed scratch" dinner) or ordering Chinese and pizza too many times a week goes against the desire to serve their families food that is wholesome and good tasting.

We are fortunate to have so many fresh and healthful foods available that just need a little dressing up to transform them into a great meal. Convenience with fresh foods has finally caught on—in the produce aisle, you can find all sorts of prewashed salad and vegetable greens, peeled and diced squash, garlic and shallots, and sliced mushrooms—someone has already done all the work for you. At the supermarket where I usually shop the variety of fresh herbs, unusual chili peppers, and previously exotic ethnic ingredients like lemongrass and sugarcane grows daily. The expanding network of farmer's markets has become the heart and soul of so many communities, where you can find all sorts of heirloom varieties and organically grown fruits and vegetables, the likes of which my grandparents were probably the last to see. These markets are also a showcase for organic meat and dairy producers and gifted artisanal bread bakers. It's possible that the greenmarket may well be the only place you shop for food.

I know that I have been influenced by the sheer abundance of foods we have now. I hope that this group of recipes, which I created in my home kitchen, will not only help cooks make the most of precious time, but also provide inspiration from the array of worldly ingredients many of us would like to explore. For curious cooks, there are many pleasures to be had by cooking and eating good, simple food. And even more when it's also quick.

About the Recipes

My goal in each recipe is to show how it's possible to make a simple and elegant meal from scratch in a reasonably short amount of time—about as long as it takes the pizza delivery to arrive at your door. (A few recipes take a little longer than the delivery guy, so save these for a weekend night.) Many of the recipes — soups and stews, noodle and pasta dishes, for instance — are hearty one-dish meals that can be served up in a bowl. Nearly all of the vegetables and salad recipes can easily be added to or rounded out to make a vegetarian supper. There are also many side dishes and dessert offerings to create a menu for a dinner party.

As an editor at *Health* magazine, I'm pretty focused on eating well and healthfully (it's my job), so I use minimal but adequate amounts of olive oil to sauté foods and light sauces to top them with; most of the cream and butter are relegated to the dessert chapter. I really like using different grains and Asian noodles instead of just plain rice and pastas—grains with attitude and power nutrients, not some dowdy dish you'd necessarily call "health food." Also, since the recipes are fairly uncomplicated, they're very adaptable to your own tastes and favorite foods: Feel free to alter most any recipe (within reason) to suit your family's particular likes and dislikes.

Cook Simple

Cook simple. For most cooks—even above-average ones—I don't think planning, shopping, and cooking is at all simple or easy. That's probably why Americans eat out on the average four nights a week (not to mention lunch) and why people are getting fatter with no end in sight. You probably don't need a study to tell you the more you eat something you made at home, the less you weigh and the better you feel. I think it's a matter of stepping back, realizing what foods you like to make, and throwing out

some old thinking about just how many ingredients you actually need to make something taste delicious. There is a middle ground between frozen dinners and four-course meals. And here it is. The point is, you don't have to cook like a chef to make great food, nor do you have to chop vegetables like one (they make food choppers and processors for that).

Read First, Cook Second

Rethink how you've always done things. Perhaps you took a cooking course or paid way too much attention to a cooking show where they drummed in the notion that you *have* to do things a certain way. In an ideal world, you would go through the list of ingredients and mince and dice each and every thing—placing them in separate little glass bowls—before you even turn on the stove. But a perfect world this isn't. Definitely read a recipe before you make it. That way, you can get things rolling—like boiling the pasta or toasting nuts—while you prepare the rest of the ingredients. Also, be aware that recipes are written by humans who sometimes make mistakes (of course, not in this book) and sometimes ask you to do steps that

aren't all that crucial (like marinating something for 8 hours when 20 minutes at room temperature will do the trick).

Many recipes in the book, like soups and stews or desserts, can be made a day or two ahead of time and assembled and reheated just before serving. Also, if you don't have the time or inclination, you can serve most of the grilled dishes without a sauce, or with a nice mustard or salsa that you purchased (I have favorites I use all the time).

Quick Kitchen Makeover

One way to streamline cooking and mealtime is to get organized, which is probably easier said than done. I'd start by spending a Saturday to really go through your kitchen—the way you might your closet, cabinet by cabinet, drawer by drawer. I'd either give away or store any pieces of cookware, tools, or equipment (when was the last time you made pasta?) I hadn't touched in a year, label the box, and put it in the garage. Next, take a look at where you keep your appliances, mixing bowls, measuring spoons and cups, and other kitchen tools. These should be stored as close as possible to the work

area near the stove, where you do most of your chopping and preparation. The point is to save some steps and reduce stress.

Purge Your Pantry

Go through your pantry items in the same way, tossing out the old cereals and grains (they turn rancid after a time). Throw away old canned goods (after two years or more) and donate the ones you're probably never

going to use. Open the spice jars and take a whiff—if the spice doesn't have a good, pungent aroma, toss it (most last six months to a year, though there are exceptions). Empty the refrigerator door's collection of vintage condiments, keeping only the ones that are fairly fresh and that you actually use on a regular basis.

Group together pantry items like spices and flavorings so you're not constantly running back and forth for things to cook with. I keep spices, divided up for savory and sweet dishes, on a double turntable, so I can just spin it around to get what I need. Place your most frequently used items—olive oil, vinegar, salt, pepper, crushed pepper, or a favorite herb—on a tray near the stove, but not so close that they'll get hot. If you don't have a good cutting board, buy a

large, sturdy one and stow it somewhere handy (mine is always on the counter next to the stove). Put only those few knives you use all the time out in the chopping block so you don't have to pull out five before you land on the one you like.

About all those gadgets . . . for years I had a giant gadget drawer—actually, I think it was *two* drawers—until I went through every item and got rid of all the silly tools I never used. Things like an apple slicer, a pasta spoon, and a cheap plastic cheese grater. I installed plastic drawer organizers (Rubbermaid), and now when I'm in the middle of cooking something, I can find what I need fast, without cutting my finger on a grapefruit sectioner. I also went through my pots and pans in the same

manner, stacking up the three skillets, two saucepans, and large pasta pot I use the most in the cabinet next to the stove. The change has been phenomenal in terms of saving time and frustration.

Here's a list of the kitchen items I've collected over the years and depend upon, and that you may want to consider acquiring:

ONE GOOD SKILLET

If you have only one thing in your kitchen, I hope it's a really great, heavy skillet with an ovenproof handle and lid. A top-of-the-line 12-inch nonstick skillet works well. You can use it for stir-frying noodle dishes or vegetables, braising stews, and browning fish or chicken before you finish cooking it in the oven. I also use it to roast chicken, cuts like rack of lamb or pork tenderloins, or a big batch of potatoes, because it cleans up better than a regular roasting pan.

CAST-IRON SKILLET

A medium-size, well-seasoned one is perfect for searing steaks; making cornbread, pineapple-upside down cakes, and fruit cobblers; grilling sandwiches and quesadillas; pan-frying chicken or fish; or for most anything you want to have a nice brown and crispy crust.

BAKING SHEETS

Large, heavy-gauge sheets you can get from a good cooking or restaurant-supply store. Don't bother scrubbing them up too well, as a good patina helps keep foods from stick-ing. I use them to roast vegetables, bake meat loaf, and hold large amounts of meats and chicken for grilling. I line them with parchment paper or aluminum foil for baking cookies.

STAINLESS STEEL SAUCEPANS

Small, medium, and large ones (2-, 4-, and 6-quart are good sizes) with tight-fitting lids. Invest in high-quality saucepans with heavy bottoms that distribute heat evenly for making rice and grain pilafs. Good pans will last a lifetime.

STOCKPOT

One large pot for making stock and soup, stewing whole chickens, and cooking pasta. An enamel-coated pot is good for tomato-based dishes.

SIEVES

Small and medium ones for straining sauces and broth, and for sifting dry ingredients for baking.

STAINLESS STEEL COLANDER

A large one for draining pasta and rinsing vegetables.

KNIVES

I don't think it's necessary to own an entire set of expensive, top-of-the-line knives, just a few good ones like a paring knife, a medium chef's knife, and a serrated bread knife.

OTHER USEFUL TOOLS AND GADGETS THAT HELP SIMPIFY

Four-sided box grater

Kitchen rasp (good for removing zest from lemons and other citrus, and for grating fresh ginger)

Garlic press

Sharp vegetable peeler (replace about every 6 months for optimum performance)

Measuring spoons, plastic cups for dry ingredients, and glass cups for liquid

A couple of wooden and metal spoons and one slotted spoon

Soup ladle

Metal whisk

Heatproof sturdy rubber spatulas

Heavy wooden rolling pin

Large, heavy cutting board

Shop Simple

I go to the supermarket during off-peak hours (early morning, after dinner) to avoid the crowds and because the shelves are usually better stocked than at peak times. I do shop on Saturdays at the farmer's market, as it's generally the best day in terms of variety (in just about any city, anywhere). I buy as much of my produce as I can in season from the green market, filling in with other things from the supermarket. The produce usually lasts the week if I wash and dry my salad greens and store them in resealeable plastic storage bags. Also, I'll use the more perishable items—like tender arugula and summer squashes—first, saving the sturdier bok choy and beets for later in the week. I like to buy fish or meat either for that day or the next, or I'll freeze some items—wrap-

ping up chicken breasts, steaks, and chops separately so I can use just one or two at a time, placing them in freezer bags with the months written on them. I shop in a little ethnic food market about once a month to restock noodles, spices, rice and beans, and sauces I can't get at the supermarket. I keep a chalkboard on the kitchen wall and jot down items as I run out of them to add to my grocery list.

A Quick Simple Pantry

These are a few of my favorite staples I like to cook with—yours are probably different, so it all depends on what your basic repertoire is. I have big metal, restaurant-type shelving with baskets and trays, and I organize things like grains, spices, and sauces separately, with the labels facing forward. You can do the same in your cupboard—the point is to have the things you reach for the most front and center, so that you can grab them quickly.

BASICS

Diamond Crystal kosher salt; white and black peppercorns; dry bread crumbs; all-purpose and cake flour; brown, confectioners', and granulated sugars; molasses and honey; good bittersweet chocolate and semisweet chips.

OILS

Extra-virgin olive oil, Asian sesame oil (refrigerate after opening), cold-pressed canola oil.

FLAVORINGS

Acidic: Red wine vinegar, seasoned rice wine vinegar, and balsamic.

Salty and piquant: White wine Worcestershire sauce, capers, anchovies and paste, Dijon-style mustard (smooth and coarse), Tabasco, and Heinz chili sauce.

Asian: Coconut milk, fish sauce, chili-garlic paste, hoisin sauce, low-sodium soy sauce (Kikkoman brand); Thai curry paste.

SPICE RACK (MOST FREQUENTLY USED)

Savory: Thyme, oregano, marjoram, bay leaf, Hungarian and Spanish paprika, Madras curry powder, crushed red pepper, cayenne, ancho chili powder, ground cumin and seeds, saffron threads.

Sweet: Chinese five-spice powder, ground coriander and seeds, ground cinnamon and sticks, fennel seeds, whole nutmegs for grating, ground mace, and ground ginger.

Pasta: Spaghetti, linguine, shells, orrechiette, whole-wheat penne and angel hair, couscous.

Asian noodles: Buckwheat soba, rice stick (cellophane), Chinese egg noodles, udon.

Rice: Jasmine, basmati, medium-grain brown rice, instant brown rice.

Grains: Yellow corn grits, quick-cooking polenta, cracked wheat (bulgur), quinoa.

Lentils: red, brown, and small green French lentils.

CANS AND CARTONS
Low-sodium chicken broth, vacuum-packed Pomi brand chopped tomatoes, chickpeas, white kidney beans, black beans, chilies in adobo, tomato paste, and Italian plum tomatoes.

PANTRY PRODUCE
Garlic, yellow onions, shallots, fresh ginger, sweet potatoes, Yukon Gold or other yellow-fleshed potatoes, and russets.

Note: Tomatoes should never be refrigerated and should be kept in a bowl, away from direct sunlight and members of the onion family.

THE REFRIGERATOR
Dairy: Eggs, milk, buttermilk, whole-milk yogurt, Parmesan, Gruyère, feta, goat cheese, and Gorgonzola.

Condiments: Hellman's light mayonnaise, kalamata and Sicilian green olives, butter, miso paste, and hot sauces.

Produce: A few things I always have on hand are lemons, limes, flat-leaf parsley, fresh bay leaf, scallions, celery, baby spinach, and romaine lettuce hearts. Bitter greens such as collard or mustard.

Note: Carrots and apples should not be stored in the same crisper as leafy greens, which would cause them to deteriorate quicker.

THE FREEZER
Vanilla ice cream; almonds and pine nuts; baby lima beans, black-eyed peas, white corn, petite peas; homemade chicken stock; slab bacon; individually wrapped chops, steaks, and chicken breasts.

Basic Vinaigrette

Quick Vinaigrette

Caesar Dressing

Miso Vinaigrette

Recipe for a Simple Salad

Easy Caesar

Tuna Steak Salad with Olive Vinaigrette

Poached Chicken, Avocado, and Citrus Salad

Tuscan Egg Salad

Warm Potato Salad with Olives and Dill

Asian Spiced Fruit

Curried Egg Salad with Olives and Capers

Cabbage, Carrot, and Chickpea Salad

Heirloom Tomato Salad with Sweet Basil Vinegar

Warm Pasta Salad with Tuna-Tomato Sauce

Spring Chopped Salad with Lime-Mint Vinaigrette

Baby Spinach with Apples and Goat Feta

Cucumber-Yogurt Salad with Ginger and Mint

Smoked Salmon and Avocado Salad

Lima Beans and Chickpeas with
Warm Bacon Dressing

Parsley Salad on Flatbread with Feta Butter

Roast Chicken–Chutney Salad

Dilled Beets and Kirby Cucumbers

Thai-Style Sausage Salad

Cold Soba Noodles

Winter Greens, Grapes, and Gorgonzola Salad

Balsamic-Shallot Vinaigrette

Cumin Chicken with Warm Black Bean Salad

salads

Just like a hearty bowl of soup, salads make wonderful suppers. Take a look in the fridge for leftover fish or chicken, potatoes, cabbage, olives, and string beans— salad doesn't have to start with lettuce. But still, a bowl of oakleaf lettuce tossed with just-snipped herbs and a light dressing is wonderful served with simple grilled chicken.

Buy prewashed greens or do it yourself in a clean sink filled with cold water and a little vinegar to remove any grit. Spin the greens dry in a salad spinner, wrap in paper towels, and store in self-sealing storage bags. They'll stay fresh and crisp for days. Make up a good vinaigrette or Caesar dressing and keep it in a jar for fresh salads all week.

Basic Vinaigrette

This is my favorite vinaigrette. Rice wine vinegar is less acidic than others, so you can use more vinegar and less oil for your salads. If you wish, add a couple of teaspoons of finely minced fresh herbs or substitute a different flavored vinegar.

Makes about 1/2 cup

1 garlic clove, finely minced

1/2 teaspoon Dijon mustard

1/4 teaspoon salt

Pinch of freshly ground black pepper

3 tablespoons seasoned rice wine vinegar

1 tablespoon fresh lemon juice (from about 1/2 lemon)

1/4 cup plus 1 tablespoon extra-virgin olive oil

In a small bowl, whisk together the garlic, mustard, salt, pepper, vinegar, and lemon juice until blended. While whisking, slowly drizzle in the oil (this helps it emulsify). The dressing will keep, refrigerated, for about 1 week.

Quick Vinaigrette

Makes 1/4 cup

3 tablespoons extra-virgin olive oil

1 tablespoon red wine vinegar or lemon juice

1 garlic clove, finely minced

Pinch of sugar

Pinch of salt

Freshly ground black pepper to taste

In a small bowl, whisk together all the ingredients or place them in a jar and shake to blend.

Caesar Dressing

Not just for Caesar salad, this dressing can be used as a hollandaise, drizzled over baked potatoes, steamed asparagus, or broccoli.

Makes 1 cup

1/4 cup light mayonnaise

1/2 cup extra-virgin olive oil

1 tablespoon fresh lemon juice (from about 1/2 lemon)

2 garlic cloves, minced or pressed through a garlic press

1 anchovy fillet

1/2 teaspoon Dijon mustard

1 teaspoon white wine Worcestershire sauce

1/4 teaspoon salt

1/4 teaspoon freshly ground black pepper

4 tablespoons freshly grated Parmesan cheese

Place all the ingredients in a blender and blend until smooth, or whisk together in a bowl. Store in a glass jar in the refrigerator (the dressing will keep for about 1 week). Shake to blend before each use.

Miso Vinaigrette

This is a light and creamy Japanese-flavored dressing that is exceptional served on grilled fish, steamed vegetables, and simple iceberg wedges.

Makes about 1 cup

6 tablespoons yellow miso (fermented soybean paste)

2 tablespoons fresh lemon juice (from about 1 lemon)

4 tablespoons fresh orange juice (from about 1/2 orange)

1 tablespoon plus 2 teaspoons grapeseed or canola oil

2 teaspoons finely grated peeled fresh ginger

1 teaspoon toasted sesame oil

2 teaspoons rice wine vinegar

Combine all the ingredients in a blender or food processor and blend until smooth. Store in a glass jar in the refrigerator (the vinaigrette will keep for about 1 week).

Recipe for a Simple Salad

Prepare a large bowl of washed and dried salad greens.

Add a handful of fresh snipped herbs such as cilantro, chives, and parsley, and some peppery greens like watercress or arugula.

Drizzle a small amount of extra-virgin olive oil over the greens and toss lightly with hands to coat.

Sprinkle with a little sea salt and freshly ground black pepper.

Shake on a few drops of red wine vinegar and toss with your hands to incorporate.

Taste.

Easy Caesar

Serves 4 to 6

6 sourdough or other crusty rolls, cut into 1-inch cubes (or 1 1/2 cups purchased croutons)

2 tablespoons extra-virgin olive oil

1/4 teaspoon salt

Pinch of freshly ground black pepper, plus more to taste

2 to 4 romaine hearts, halved or chopped

1/4 cup Caesar Dressing (page 19)

Parmesan cheese for shaving

Preheat the oven to 350°F.

In a small bowl, combine the sourdough pieces with the olive oil. Toss and season with the salt and pepper. Spread on a baking sheet and bake for 10 to 12 minutes, or until golden.

Place the romaine hearts on a serving platter and drizzle with the dressing. Top with Parmesan shavings and the croutons, and season to taste with additional pepper.

QUICK SIMPLE IDEA

You can find romaine hearts, which require no washing or trimming, in the packaged salad section. Simply slice off the ends and quarter or chop to suit your salad.

Tuna Steak Salad with Olive Vinaigrette

Serves 2

1 6- to 8-ounce tuna steak (about 1¼-inch thick)

Pinch of salt and freshly ground black pepper

1 teaspoon plus 3 tablespoons extra-virgin olive oil

1 tablespoon red wine vinegar

1 garlic clove, minced

10 kalamata olives, pitted and halved

¼ teaspoon crumbled dried thyme or marjoram

1 large bunch of arugula or watercress, tough stems removed, washed, and spun dry

2 plum tomatoes, thinly sliced

Sprinkle the tuna on both sides with salt and pepper. In a nonstick skillet over a medium-high flame, heat 1 teaspoon of the oil. Sear the tuna on both sides, 2 to 3 minutes per side for medium, or longer if desired. Transfer to a cutting board and let rest.

Add the remaining 3 tablespoons of oil, the vinegar, garlic, olives, and thyme to the skillet and heat, stirring, for about 1 minute. Remove from the heat. Slice the tuna crosswise into ¼-inch-thick pieces. Divide the greens and tomatoes between 2 plates. Place the tuna on top of the greens, spoon the olives and vinaigrette over the salads, and serve while the dressing and tuna are still warm.

Poached Chicken, Avocado, and Citrus Salad

Serves 4 to 6

6 tablespoons extra-virgin olive oil

2 tablespoons sherry or red wine vinegar

2 tablespoons fresh orange juice (from about $1/2$ orange)

Pinch of salt, plus more to taste

Pinch of freshly ground black pepper, plus more to taste

4 skinless, boneless chicken breast halves (about 1 pound)

4 blood oranges or 2 navel oranges

1 small red onion, thinly sliced (about 1 cup), rinsed and drained

1 large or 2 small heads oakleaf lettuce greens, washed and spun dry

2 firm-ripe Hass avocados, peeled, pitted, and sliced

Bring a large pot of lightly salted water to a boil. In a small bowl, whisk together the oil, vinegar, orange juice, salt, and pepper. Add the chicken breasts to the boiling water, reduce the heat to medium, and simmer for about 10 minutes, or until the chicken is no longer pink inside. Remove the chicken and cool for 5 minutes on a cutting board, then slice into long strips. Transfer the chicken to a bowl and toss with a few tablespoons of the dressing. Season to taste with salt and pepper.

With a sharp knife, remove the orange peel and white pith from the oranges. Slice the oranges crosswise into thin rounds. In a large bowl, toss the onion and lettuce with the remaining vinaigrette. Divide among serving bowls and top with the chicken, oranges, and avocado.

QUICK SIMPLE IDEA

You can also make the salad using ruby red grapefruit sections. In the summer, instead of poaching, brush the chicken breasts with a little of the vinaigrette and grill them.

Tuscan Egg Salad

Serves 4

12 large eggs, beaten

1 tablespoon extra-virgin olive oil

1 large shallot, chopped

2 tablespoons salted butter

1/2 cup cherry tomato halves

2 tablespoons freshly grated Parmesan cheese

2 cups mixed greens, such as arugula and frisée, or mesclun

Salt and freshly ground black pepper to taste

In a large bowl, beat the eggs. Heat the oil in a nonstick skillet over a medium flame and sauté the shallots for about 1 minute, or until wilted. Add the eggs and butter and stir over the heat until the eggs are cooked but still soft and creamy, 3 to 5 minutes. Remove from the heat and toss with the tomatoes, Parmesan, and greens. Season to taste with salt and pepper, and serve hot.

QUICK SIMPLE IDEA

Creamy scrambled eggs combined with fresh tomatoes and greens are best eaten seconds after the eggs are finished. You can also add crisp crumbled bacon, or substitute your favorite cheese.

Warm Potato Salad with Olives and Dill

Serves 6 to 8

2 pounds Yukon Gold potatoes, scrubbed

Salt

2 garlic cloves, minced

1 teaspoon dried oregano

2 tablespoons fresh lemon juice (from about 1 lemon)

4 tablespoons white vinegar

1/3 cup extra-virgin olive oil

1/4 teaspoon freshly ground black pepper, plus more to taste

1/2 cup kalamata or other brine-cured olives, pitted and halved

1 medium red onion, thinly sliced

3 tablespoons minced fresh dill

3/4 cup (2 ounces) crumbled feta cheese (the best quality you can find), optional

Place the potatoes in a large pot and cover with cold water. Bring to a boil and salt the water. Cook until just tender, about 20 minutes. When cool enough to handle, peel and thinly slice.

Meanwhile, combine the garlic, oregano, lemon juice, vinegar, oil, 1 teaspoon salt, and pepper to taste in a blender or food processor and purée until smooth. Place in a large bowl with the olives, onion, and dill. Add the potatoes, toss to combine, and fold in the feta, if using. Add more salt and pepper to taste, and serve warm, at room temperature, or chilled.

QUICK SIMPLE IDEA

This is a light-style potato salad, fragrant with dill and lemon. Instead of feta, it is also good topped with imported canned tuna in olive oil.

Asian Spiced Fruit

Southeast Asian cooks have a great talent for juxtaposing flavors like sweet, hot, and spicy to create unexpected taste combinations. Serve this as a palate-cleansing salad or as a side dish to spicy grilled meat or fish. It makes a deliciously exotic dessert spooned over coconut sorbet.

Serves 6 to 8

$1/3$ cup fresh-squeezed orange juice (from about $1^1/2$ oranges)

2 tablespoons honey, or to taste

3 tablespoons fresh lime juice (from 2 limes)

$1^1/2$ tablespoons finely minced, peeled fresh gingerroot

1 to 2 small red chilies, seeded and finely minced

$1/4$ teaspoon ground white pepper

$1/2$ teaspoon ground cinnamon

$1/4$ teaspoon ground cardamom

2 ripe mangoes, peeled, seeded, and diced

2 ripe red bananas (or 4 baby bananas), peeled and diced

1 large ripe papaya, peeled, seeded, and diced

2 ripe peaches, peeled and diced

$1/2$ ripe fresh pineapple, peeled, cored, and diced

$1/4$ cup slivered fresh mint leaves

In a small bowl, whisk together the orange juice, honey, lime juice, ginger, chilies, pepper, cinnamon, and cardamom. Toss with all the fruit in a serving bowl. Serve immediately or cover the bowl with plastic wrap and refrigerate for 1 to 2 hours to intensify the flavors. Top with the mint leaves before serving.

Curried Egg Salad with Olives and Capers

8 large hard-boiled eggs

3 tablespoons finely chopped red onion

2 tablespoons drained capers

6 kalamata olives, pitted and finely chopped

1 tablespoon minced fresh dill

4 tablespoons light mayonnaise

1 teaspoon fresh lemon juice

½ teaspoon curry powder

½ teaspoon salt

¼ teaspoon freshly ground black pepper

Remove the egg shells and chop the eggs fine. Combine in a medium bowl with the onion, capers, olives, dill, mayonnaise, lemon juice, curry powder, and salt and pepper. Stir to combine. The egg salad can be prepared to this point, placed in a sealed container, and refrigerated until ready to serve.

QUICK SIMPLE IDEA

Serve the egg salad on toasted pumpernickel bread or pita wedges with sprigs of watercress.

Cabbage, Carrot, and Chickpea Salad

Serves 6 to 8

Dressing

⅓ cup apple cider vinegar

1 tablespoon canola or grapeseed oil

1 tablespoon finely minced fresh ginger

2 tablespoons honey

½ teaspoon crushed red pepper

½ teaspoon salt

Salad

1 small head Savoy or Napa cabbage

1 small head radicchio, thinly sliced

1 cup shredded carrots

1 small red onion, thinly sliced

4 large red radishes, thinly sliced

½ red bell pepper, seeded and thinly sliced

1 14½-ounce can chickpeas, rinsed and drained

In a large bowl, whisk together the dressing ingredients. With a large sharp knife, slice the cabbage in half and cut out the heart. Thinly slice crosswise to shred. Place in a large bowl with the radicchio, carrots, onion, radishes, bell pepper, and chickpeas. Whisk the dressing again and toss with the salad. Chill for at least 30 minutes before serving.

QUICK SIMPLE IDEA

An inexpensive plastic Asian slicer (it works like a mandoline) will make quick work of the vegetables.

Heirloom Tomato Salad with Sweet Basil Vinegar

Serves 4 to 6

3 pounds small heirloom (or other) tomatoes

1/2 cup loosely packed opal basil leaves (or other basil), plus more for garnish

1/2 cup seasoned rice wine or champagne vinegar

1/2 teaspoon minced garlic

1 teaspoon sugar

Salt and freshly ground black pepper to taste

Thinly slice the tomatoes and arrange on a platter with half of the basil leaves. Combine the remaining ingredients in a blender and purée until liquefied. Strain, pour over the tomatoes, and refrigerate until ready to serve. (The salad will stay fresh-tasting for up to 3 hours.)

QUICK SIMPLE IDEA

Choose whatever tomatoes are in season and ripest. Heirloom, grape, or other smallish tomatoes —or a mixture—make a pretty and tasty salad. If you can find heirloom tomatoes at a farmer's market, you will often find opal basil from a vender nearby. If not, Italian or Thai basil are equally good.

Warm Pasta Salad with Tuna-Tomato Sauce

Serves 4

1/2 pound cappelletti or shell pasta

Two 6-ounce cans tuna packed in olive oil (preferably Progresso or an Italian brand), drained

1 1/4 cups cherry tomatoes, halved

1/4 cup extra-virgin olive oil

2 tablespoons red wine vinegar

1 shallot, finely chopped

3 tablespoons minced flat-leaf parsley

1 teaspoon dried thyme or oregano

1/2 teaspoon salt

1/4 teaspoon freshly ground black pepper, plus more to taste

3 tablespoons drained capers

3 ounces Parmesan cheese

Cook the pasta in a pot of boiling salted water until al dente. Transfer to a large bowl and toss with the tuna and tomatoes. Whisk together the oil, vinegar, shallot, parsley, thyme, and salt and pepper. Drizzle over the pasta, add the capers, and toss. Adjust seasonings, divide among 4 bowls, shave or grate Parmesan over the top, and add more ground pepper to taste.

Spring Chopped Salad with Lime-Mint Vinaigrette

Serves 4

1¹/₂ cups thinly sliced fennel or celery heart

2 firm-ripe Hass avocados, peeled and cut into
   ¹/₂-inch dice

2 large hard-boiled eggs, chopped

4 scallions (white and green parts), chopped

³/₄ cup thinly sliced radishes

1 cup small (French) string beans (haricots verts),
   steamed tender and halved

4 cups watercress, tough stems removed

1¹/₂ cups flat-leaf parsley, long stems removed

2 tablespoons fresh lime juice (from about
   2 limes)

4 tablespoons extra-virgin olive oil

2 tablespoons thinly slivered fresh mint leaves

Salt and freshly ground black pepper

In a large bowl, combine the fennel, avocados, eggs, scallions, radishes, string beans, watercress, and parsley. Whisk together the lime juice, oil, and mint and add salt and pepper to taste. Toss with the salad ingredients.

Baby Spinach with Apples and Goat Feta

Serves 4

2 Golden Delicious apples (unpeeled), cored and cut into large dice

4 tablespoons lemon juice (from about 2 lemons)

10 cups prewashed baby spinach leaves (about 2 5-ounce packages)

3 tablespoons extra-virgin olive oil

1 tablespoon apple cider vinegar

2 tablespoons honey

$1/2$ teaspoon salt

Pinch of freshly ground black pepper

$3/4$ cup pecan pieces, toasted

8 ounces goat feta or blue-veined goat cheese, broken into big chunks

Toss the apples with 2 tablespoons of the lemon juice. Place the spinach in a large salad bowl and remove long stems and any bruised leaves. Whisk together the remaining 2 tablespoons of lemon juice, the olive oil, vinegar, honey, salt, and pepper. Toss the spinach and apples with just enough vinaigrette to coat. Divide among 4 plates, top with the nuts, and place chunks of cheese on the side.

QUICK SIMPLE IDEA

Goat feta tastes fresher and less salty than traditional Greek feta, and it is very good simply drizzled with a little olive oil on toasted bread or crackers.

Cucumber-Yogurt Salad with Ginger and Mint

This salad makes a good side dish with spicy grilled chicken or fish. It's thick and flavorful with ginger and bell pepper.

Serves 4 to 6

1¼ cups plain whole-milk yogurt

1 tablespoon olive oil

1 red bell pepper, seeded and diced

3 teaspoons finely grated fresh ginger

4 scallions, thinly sliced (white and green parts)

1 English (hothouse) cucumber, peeled, quartered, and diced

3 tablespoons slivered mint leaves

Salt and freshly ground black pepper to taste

Place the yogurt in a fine-mesh strainer over a small bowl and drain for 20 minutes. In a large nonstick skillet, heat the oil over a medium flame. Add the bell pepper and ginger and sauté for 2 to 3 minutes, until the pepper is soft. Remove from the heat and stir in the scallions. Set aside to cool (or transfer to a bowl and place in the freezer for 10 minutes).

Toss the bell pepper–scallion mixture with the cucumber, mint, and strained yogurt. Season to taste with salt and pepper. Chill for about 30 minutes (or longer) before serving. The salad is best served the same day.

Smoked Salmon and Avocado Salad

Serves 4

1 ripe Hass avocado, pitted, peeled, and thinly sliced

12 ounces sliced smoked salmon

1 Kirby cucumber, thinly sliced lengthwise with a vegetable peeler

½ cup thinly sliced red onion (about 1 small onion), rinsed and drained

2 tablespoons capers, drained

2 teaspoons finely minced fresh dill

1 teaspoon finely grated lemon zest

2 tablespoons fresh lemon juice (from about 1 lemon)

2 tablespoons extra-virgin olive oil

On a large chilled platter, arrange the avocado slices in one layer. Top with loosely folded slices of salmon, then the cucumber slices, followed by the onion rings. Scatter the capers over the top. In a small bowl, whisk together the dill, zest, lemon juice, and olive oil, and drizzle over the salad.

Lima Beans and Chickpeas with Warm Bacon Dressing

You can use most any beans in this salad—edamame and black-eyed peas are also good with the bacon dressing. It's also a nice meal served with hot white or brown rice.

Serves 6 to 8

2 10-ounce packages frozen baby lima beans

4 pieces thick-sliced bacon, chopped

2 small leeks (white and light green parts), sliced and thoroughly rinsed

3 garlic cloves, minced

3 tablespoons extra-virgin olive oil

4 tablespoons sherry vinegar

2 teaspoons minced fresh thyme leaves

Salt and freshly ground black pepper to taste

1 14$\frac{1}{2}$-ounce can chickpeas, rinsed and drained

Cook the lima beans in a small amount of boiling salted water until tender, 10 to 12 minutes. Drain and rinse in a colander beneath cold running water.

In a large nonstick skillet over medium heat, cook the bacon, stirring, until crisp; remove with a slotted spoon and drain on paper towels. Add the leeks and garlic to the bacon fat and cook, stirring, until the leeks are soft. Drain off all but 1 tablespoon of the drippings. Whisk the olive oil with the vinegar, thyme, and salt and pepper. Add to the pan and heat for 1 minute. Combine the leeks and vinaigrette with the lima beans and chickpeas and toss. Top with the bacon bits and serve.

Parsley Salad on Flatbread with Feta Butter

Serves 4 to 6

1/2 medium Vidalia onion, thinly sliced

1/4 cup Quick Vinaigrette (page 18)

1 garlic clove, minced

3 medium tomatoes, seeded and diced

6 medium Kirby cucumbers (or 1 1/2 hothouse or English cucumbers), peeled and diced

4 cups roughly chopped flat-leaf parsley

3 tablespoons minced fresh dill

Salt and freshly ground black pepper

4 to 6 large pieces thin flatbread, such as lavash

Feta Butter (recipe follows), optional

Rinse the onion beneath cold running water and drain. Toss it with the vinaigrette and let sit for 10 minutes. Add the garlic, tomatoes, cucumbers, and herbs and toss lightly. Season with salt and pepper to taste. Chill until ready to serve. Serve on flatbread spread with about 2 tablespoons of Feta Butter.

Feta Butter
Makes about 1 1/4 cups

4 ounces Neufchâtel (reduced-fat) cream cheese, at room temperature

4 tablespoons (1/2 stick) unsalted butter, at room temperature

3/4 cup crumbled feta cheese

2 tablespoons minced fresh mint

2 tablespoons minced fresh chives

Salt to taste

Combine all the ingredients in a small bowl and stir with a fork until creamy. The butter will keep, refrigerated, for up to 1 week.

QUICK SIMPLE IDEA

This delicious butter is also good as a spread for tomato sandwiches or served on crackers.

Roast Chicken–Chutney Salad

This quick and easy chicken salad is best made with a freshly roasted chicken and served straightaway.

Serves 3 to 4

1¼- to 1½-pound rotisserie chicken (should yield about 4 cups chicken meat)

½ cup diced celery (about 2 ribs)

¼ cup finely diced onion (about ½ medium onion)

½ cup red grapes, halved (optional)

⅓ cup chopped flat-leaf parsley

¼ cup chopped pecans, toasted

⅓ cup light mayonnaise

1 tablespoon fresh lemon juice (from about ½ lemon)

2 tablespoons Major Grey (mango-ginger) chutney

Salt and freshly ground black pepper to taste

Remove the skin and bone the chicken. Tear into small (½-inch) pieces; discard the skin and bones. Toss the chicken with the celery, onion, grapes, parsley, and pecans. Stir in the mayonnaise, lemon juice, and chutney. Season to taste with salt and pepper. Serve immediately or refrigerate until ready to serve (the salad is best served immediately but will stay fresh for about 2 days).

QUICK SIMPLE IDEA

If the chutney you buy seems unusually thick and chunky, dice up the larger pieces before adding it to the salad.

Dilled Beets and Kirby Cucumbers

Serves 4

1 tablespoon extra-virgin olive oil, plus more for brushing

1 pound (4 to 5 medium) beets, scrubbed and quartered

4 small to medium Kirby cucumbers, quartered

2 tablespoons coarsely chopped fresh dill

1 small red onion, sliced into rings

2 teaspoons balsamic vinegar (or more to taste)

Salt and freshly ground black pepper

Heat the oven to 425°F. Line a baking sheet with two sheets of foil and lightly oil the top sheet. Place the beets cut-side down on the foil. Fold the foil tightly around the beets and roast for 25 to 30 minutes, until fork-tender. Once cool, peel and slice.

Place the beets in a bowl with the cucumbers, dill, and onion. Drizzle with the olive oil, a little balsamic, and salt and pepper to taste. Toss and chill until ready to serve.

Thai-Style Sausage Salad

Serves 4 to 6

1 pound hot or sweet Italian sausages (or other
   spicy sausage), casings on, thinly sliced

2 tablespoons fresh lime juice (from 1 to
   2 limes)

1 tablespoon seasoned rice wine vinegar

1 tablespoon low-sodium soy sauce

1 teaspoon sugar

1 small red onion, thinly sliced

1 red serrano chili, thinly sliced

1/2 cup coarsely chopped fresh cilantro leaves

1/2 cup torn Thai (or Italian) basil leaves

1/2 head romaine lettuce heart, shredded

In a large nonstick skillet over medium-high
heat, place the sausages and brown on all
sides, stirring, 5 to 8 minutes, until cooked
through. Set aside and keep warm.

In a large bowl, whisk together the lime
juice, vinegar, soy sauce, and sugar. Toss the
sausages with the dressing, onion, chili,
cilantro, and basil. Arrange the lettuce on a
platter and top with the sausage mixture.

Cold Soba Noodles

Serves 4 to 6

4 tablespoons low-sodium soy sauce

4 tablespoons seasoned rice wine vinegar

1 teaspoon sugar

1 tablespoon fresh lemon juice (from about
   1/2 lemon)

Dash of toasted sesame oil

8 ounces soba (thin buckwheat) noodles

4 scallions, thinly sliced (white and light green
   parts)

1/2 English cucumber, seeded and thinly sliced

6 large radishes, thinly sliced

In a small bowl, combine the soy sauce, vinegar, sugar, lemon juice, and sesame oil and whisk until well blended. Bring a pot of salted water to a boil and cook the soba noodles until just tender but not mushy, 3 to 4 minutes. Drain and rinse under cold water until cool. Drain well. In a large bowl, combine the noodles, scallions, cucumber, and radishes. Toss with the soy dressing and serve at room temperature or chilled.

QUICK SIMPLE IDEA

Soba noodles are made with buckwheat flour and have a delicate texture and subtle earthy flavor. Add cooked small shrimps or sautéed, thinly sliced shiitake mushroom caps for a heartier noodle dinner.

Winter Greens, Grapes, and Gorgonzola Salad

This is an elegant salad to serve for a dinner party (or just for yourself). You can substitute ripe pears, mangoes, persimmons, and even pomegranate seeds for the grapes.

Serves 4 to 6

1 head red-leaf or green Bibb lettuce, leaves separated

½ small head radicchio (about 5 ounces), leaves separated

1 small bulb fennel, very thinly sliced

1 cup seedless black or red grapes, halved

3 to 4 tablespoons Balsamic-Shallot Vinaigrette (recipe follows)

½ cup walnut pieces or chopped hazelnuts, toasted

4 ounces Gorgonzola, Saga Blue, or other blue cheese, thinly sliced

Place the Bibb and radicchio in a large salad bowl. Top with the fennel and grapes. Toss with the vinaigrette, then top with the nuts and Gorgonzola.

Balsamic-Shallot Vinaigrette
Makes about 1 cup

1 shallot, minced

½ teaspoon salt

¼ teaspoon freshly ground black pepper

3 tablespoons balsamic vinegar

4 tablespoons grapeseed oil (or cold-pressed canola oil)

4 tablespoons extra-virgin olive oil

In a small bowl, whisk together the shallot, salt, pepper, and vinegar. As you whisk, slowly drizzle in the oils until emulsified. The vinaigrette will stay fresh, refrigerated, for about 1 week. Shake to blend before each use.

Cumin Chicken with Warm Black Bean Salad

Serves 4

4 boneless, skinless chicken breast halves

1½ teaspoons ground cumin

¼ teaspoon cayenne pepper, plus more to taste

½ teaspoon salt, plus more to taste

¼ teaspoon freshly ground black pepper, plus more to taste

1 tablespoon plus 2 teaspoons olive oil

½ cup onion (about ½ medium onion)

2 garlic cloves, minced

15-ounce can black beans, rinsed and drained

1 cup fresh white corn kernels, or frozen, thawed

1½ cups cherry tomatoes, halved

1 tablespoon red wine vinegar

4 scallions (white and green parts), thinly sliced

½ cup coarsely chopped fresh cilantro leaves, plus more for garnish

4 to 8 warm, buttered corn tortillas (optional)

Place the chicken breasts between 2 sheets of plastic wrap and pound with a mallet or the bottom of a heavy skillet to a ½-inch thickness. In a small bowl, combine the cumin, cayenne, salt, and pepper and rub evenly over the chicken. In a large nonstick skillet, heat 1 tablespoon of the oil over a medium flame. Sauté the chicken for 4 minutes per side, until cooked through. Remove to a cutting board and let rest for 5 minutes.

In the same skillet, sauté the onion and garlic in the remaining 2 teaspoons of oil over medium heat for 2 minutes, until softened. Add the beans, corn, tomatoes, and 3 tablespoons of water and cook, stirring, for 1 to 2 minutes, until just heated through. Remove from the heat and toss with the vinegar, scallions, and cilantro. Season to taste with additional salt, pepper, and cayenne. Slice each chicken piece crosswise and arrange on top of the beans. Serve with tortillas, if desired.

White Corn Pudding Bread

Curried Okra and Tomatoes

Asparagus with Prosciutto-Bacon and Eggs

Broccoli Raab Bruschetta

Simple Pesto

Ratatouille

Green Thai Vegetable Curry

Eggplant Stacks

Curried Eggplant Omelet with Dill and Tomatoes

Stir-Fried Greens and Basil

Grilled Tomato-Corn Salsa

Roasted Eggplant Spread

Grilled Mexican Corn

Simple Mashed Potatoes
WASABI MASHED POTATOES
BASIL MASHED POTATOES
GARLIC MASHED POTATOES WITH PEAS

Salt-Baked Crushed Potatoes
with Lentils and Fried Onions

Oven Frites

Sweet Potato–Chipotle Pancakes

Baked Sweet Potatoes

vegetables

Sometimes a steaming baked sweet potato sprinkled with brown sugar and butter is all you really want for dinner. Gone are the days when a proper meal always meant meat, chicken, or fish anchored by a starch and a green vegetable. Vegetables make good, hearty dinners all by themselves. Meaty mushrooms, thick slabs of eggplant, glorious starchy roots, and mashed potatoes are the basis of many wonderful meals. Summer vegetables may be the most inspiring of all, and hunting and gathering is half the fun—fill the backseat of your car with baskets of fresh vegetables from the farmer's market (or from the guy by the side of the road with a garden's worth in his pickup). Cucumbers, okra, tomatoes, peppers, string beans, and a baker's dozen bag of corn (is it possible to eat too much corn?) require only minuscule amounts of vinegar, extra-virgin olive oil or melted butter, and a pinch of sea salt to enhance their sun-ripened flavors. Don't even wait to get home to enjoy a taste. Bite into a dead-ripe tomato as you drive along and let the juice run down your chin.

White Corn Pudding Bread

Serves 6 to 8

2 tablespoons (1/4 stick) unsalted butter, melted, plus more for greasing skillet

1 cup white cornmeal

2 tablespoons sugar

1 teaspoon baking soda

1/2 teaspoon salt

1 1/2 cups buttermilk

4 ounces cream cheese, softened

3 large eggs

3 cups fresh white corn kernels (4 to 6 ears uncooked corn) or 3 cups frozen white corn kernels, thawed

Preheat the oven to 350°F. Butter a 10-inch iron skillet or a 9-inch glass pie dish.

In a large mixing bowl, combine the cornmeal, sugar, baking soda, and salt. In a blender or food processor, combine the melted butter, buttermilk, cream cheese, and eggs. Purée until smooth. Add the corn and pulse a few times (the mixture should be lumpy, with visible kernels). Add the corn mixture to the cornmeal mixture and stir until well blended. Pour into the prepared skillet or pie dish and bake for 30 to 35 minutes, until the center is just firm to the touch and the bread is golden brown around the edges. Transfer to a rack to cool, then cut into 6 to 8 wedges. Serve warm or at room temperature.

QUICK SIMPLE IDEA

A cross between corn bread and pudding, this moist bread takes advantage of summer's sweet corn. If you can't find white corn or cornmeal, you can substitute yellow. Slice into wedges and top with a Grilled Tomato-Corn Salsa (page 57).

Curried Okra
and Tomatoes

Serves 4

1 pound okra

1½ tablespoons extra-virgin olive oil

Pinch of crushed red pepper

½ teaspoon ground cumin

½ teaspoon ground coriander

2 garlic cloves, minced

1 small red onion, thinly sliced

1 large ripe tomato, coarsely chopped

1 teaspoon sugar

4 large basil leaves, slivered

2 tablespoons coarsely chopped fresh cilantro

Salt and freshly ground black pepper

¼ lime

Trim the tips of the stem end of the okra (but not the pointed end) and halve lengthwise. Place the oil in a large skillet over medium-high heat. Add the pepper flakes, cumin, and coriander and stir-fry for 30 seconds. Stir in the garlic and onion and cook until soft, about 3 minutes. Add the okra and 2 tablespoons of water. Cover tightly and allow to steam for 3 to 4 minutes, until the okra is bright green and crisp-tender. Remove the lid and add the tomato, sugar, basil, and cilantro. Cook, stirring once, for about 30 seconds (very little stirring keeps the okra from becoming slimy). Remove from the heat and season with salt and pepper and a squeeze of lime juice.

QUICK SIMPLE IDEA

Select petite okra pods, which are the tastiest and most tender. Small pods also cook much more quickly and won't become viscous. Try this with cubed smoked tofu and serve it with saffron rice.

Asparagus with Prosciutto-Bacon and Eggs

Serves 4

Extra-virgin olive oil

8 ounces thinly sliced prosciutto

1 pound asparagus

Salt and freshly ground black pepper

2 large hard-boiled eggs, coarsely chopped

Preheat the oven to 400°F.

Lightly brush a large baking sheet with oil. Arrange the prosciutto slices and bake, watching carefully, until the prosciutto is very crisp, 10 to 12 minutes. Cool and crumble into large pieces.

Meanwhile, snap off the tough ends of the asparagus (if the spears are large, peel the ends). Bring a large deep skillet filled with salted water to a boil. Add the asparagus and simmer over medium heat until crisp-tender and still bright green, 3 to 5 minutes. Drain, drizzle with a little olive oil, and season to taste with salt and pepper. Arrange on a platter and top with the chopped eggs and prosciutto.

QUICK SIMPLE IDEA

Baking prosciutto makes it crisp like bacon, only sans the fat. Crumble it over salads and vegetables, and add to scrambled eggs.

Broccoli Raab Bruschetta

The crusty Italian toasts used in this recipe are the ultimate in garlic bread to serve with any meal.

Serves 4

2 bunches broccoli raab (about 1¹/₂ pounds), tough stems removed, coarsely chopped

3 tablespoons extra-virgin olive oil

3 garlic cloves, minced

¹/₄ teaspoon crushed red pepper

Salt and freshly ground black pepper

¹/₂ loaf crusty Italian bread, cut into 8 ¹/₂-inch-thick slices

2 garlic cloves, halved

Parmesan cheese for shaving

Bring a large pot of salted water to a boil. Add the broccoli raab and cook for about 5 minutes, until tender but still bright green; drain and gently squeeze excess water. In a large skillet, heat 2 tablespoons of the oil over a medium flame. Add the minced garlic and red pepper and cook until fragrant, for a few seconds (do not burn). Add the broccoli raab and toss to coat. Season with salt and pepper to taste. Set aside, and keep warm.

Preheat the broiler or a grill. Place the bread on a large baking sheet about 5 inches beneath the broiler. Toast (or grill) on both sides, about 3 minutes (watch carefully). When cool enough to handle, rub one side of each slice with the cut side of the halved garlic cloves. Sprinkle the bread with salt and pepper and drizzle lightly with the remaining tablespoon of olive oil. Spoon the broccoli raab on toasts, top with shaved Parmesan, and serve while still warm.

Simple Pesto

This is a very easy recipe for pesto. It's best used immediately—toss it with hot cooked pasta or steamed fresh string beans.

Makes about 1¹/₂ cups

3 garlic cloves

3 cups loosely packed fresh basil

1 cup loosely packed Italian flat-leaf parsley

¹/₄ cup toasted pine nuts

¹/₂ cup grated Parmesan cheese

³/₄ cup extra-virgin olive oil

¹/₄ teaspoon salt

With the motor of a blender or food processor running, drop in the garlic cloves and mince well. Add the basil, parsley, pine nuts, and cheese, and pulse to chop the ingredients. With the motor running, slowly pour in the oil and process until the mixture is smooth. Season with the salt. Use immediately or transfer to a glass jar and cover with a little olive oil before sealing. The pesto will keep, refrigerated, for about 1 week.

Ratatouille

Ratatouille must be the ultimate vegetable meal. Here's a quick and tasty version that cooks in less than 15 minutes. Try it with hot buttered egg noodles or steamed rice.

Serves 4 to 6

2 tablespoons vegetable oil

2 garlic cloves, minced

1 large red onion, thickly sliced

1 medium eggplant, diced

2 small zucchini, diced

1 red bell pepper, cut into large dice

¹/₂ teaspoon salt, plus more to taste

¹/₄ teaspoon freshly ground black pepper, plus more to taste

¹/₃ cup low-sodium chicken or vegetable broth

Pinch of cayenne, or more to taste

2 to 4 teaspoons apple cider vinegar or fresh lemon juice

2 tablespoons coarsely chopped fresh cilantro leaves

In a large nonstick skillet or wok, heat the oil. Add the garlic and onion and stir-fry for 1 minute. Cover and steam for 3 minutes, until the onion is soft. Add the eggplant, zucchini, and bell pepper and stir to coat. Season with the salt and pepper. Add the broth, cover, and steam for 8 to 10 minutes, until crisp-tender. Sprinkle with the cayenne, vinegar, and cilantro and serve.

Green Thai Vegetable Curry

Pleasantly spicy with a creamy coconut base, this curry is heady with chili, ginger, and lemongrass. Serve it with fragrant jasmine rice. Kaffir lime leaves really complete the curry—you can find them frozen at Asian markets.

Serves 4 to 6

1 tablespoon vegetable oil

1 medium onion, chopped

2 to 3 garlic cloves, minced

1 small Thai or serrano chili, thinly sliced

2 teaspoons peeled and minced fresh ginger

2 teaspoons green Thai curry paste (preferably Mae Ploy brand)

3 cups light unsweetened canned coconut milk

$1/2$ cup low-sodium chicken or vegetable broth

1 2-inch stalk lemongrass, lightly pounded with a mallet

2 Japanese eggplants ($1/2$ pound), cut into $1/2$-inch-thick slices, steamed until tender

3 ounces small string beans, trimmed, halved, and steamed until tender

3 plum tomatoes, seeded and sliced $1/2$-inch thick

Salt

2 Kaffir lime leaves or 2 teaspoons fresh lime juice (from about 1 lime)

$1/4$ cup slivered Thai or Italian basil leaves

In a large, deep saucepan or wok, heat the oil over medium-high heat. Stir-fry the onion, garlic, chilies, and ginger until soft, about 3 minutes. In a small bowl, whisk together the curry paste with $1/2$ cup of coconut milk and add to the pan along with the remaining coconut milk, chicken broth, and lemongrass. Bring to a boil, reduce the heat to low, and simmer for 10 minutes. Add the eggplants, beans, and tomatoes and simmer for 3 minutes. Season with salt and stir in the lime leaves (or juice) and basil. Serve the curry in shallow bowls with a scoop of rice.

VARIATION: VEGETABLE AND SHRIMP CURRY
Add 6 ounces shelled and deveined large shrimp along with the tomatoes and simmer for 3 to 5 minutes, until the shrimp are bright pink.

Eggplant Stacks

Serves 2

3 tablespoons extra-virgin olive oil

1 tablespoon minced fresh rosemary

1 garlic clove, minced

$1/2$ teaspoon salt

$1/4$ teaspoon freshly ground black pepper

1 $1^1/2$- to 2-pound eggplant, trimmed and cut
   into 6 $1/2$-inch-thick slices

4 $1/4$-inch-thick slices fresh mozzarella
   (about 4 ounces)

1 large beefsteak tomato, cut into 4 thick slices

4 large basil leaves, plus more for garnish

$1/4$ cup Simple Pesto (page 50), optional

Heat the grill to medium (or the oven to
400°F.). In a blender or food processor,
combine the olive oil, rosemary, garlic, salt,
pepper, and 2 tablespoons of water. Purée.

Brush the eggplant slices with the olive oil
mixture and let stand for 5 minutes. Grill,
turning occasionally, until they just begin to
soften (or bake on a greased baking sheet
for 12 to 15 minutes). Place the cheese on
4 slices. Put the tomato slices on a piece of
aluminum foil on top of the grill to warm.
When the cheese begins to melt, transfer the
eggplant slices to a platter. Top the cheese
slices with a basil leaf and a warm tomato
slice. Top each with another cheese-topped
eggplant slice and tomato. Top both with a
basil leaf and a plain eggplant slice. Drizzle
with a little pesto, if desired. Serve hot.

QUICK SIMPLE IDEA

This is a perfect summer appetizer or meal with a
salad and grilled garlic bread. You can double—or
triple—the recipe for a dinner party. Precook the
eggplant, warm in a 350°F. oven, and then top
with the cheese. Remember to warm the tomato
slices before assembling.

Curried Eggplant Omelet with Dill and Tomatoes

Serves 4

1 small eggplant (3/4 to 1 pound)

2 teaspoons salt, plus more to taste

2 tablespoons olive oil

1 large onion, sliced

1/4 teaspoon freshly ground black pepper

1/4 teaspoon ground turmeric

3 teaspoons minced fresh dill

6 large eggs, beaten

3 medium tomatoes, seeded and chopped

4 tablespoons plain Greek-style yogurt or sour cream

Trim the ends from the eggplant and cut into 3/4-inch cubes (you should have about 4 cups). Place the cubes in a colander, sprinkle with 2 teaspoons salt, and let stand for 10 minutes. Rinse with cool water and squeeze out most of the water with your hands (this is important).

Preheat the broiler to high. In a 9- or 10-inch nonstick ovenproof skillet over a medium flame, heat the oil. Add the onion, pepper, and turmeric and sauté until the onion is soft, 3 to 5 minutes. Add the eggplant and sauté until browned and soft, 5 to 8 minutes. Sprinkle with the dill, add the eggs, sprinkle with a large pinch of salt, and stir briefly to combine. Stir 1 or 2 times more, until the eggs begin to cook. Cover and cook 1 to 3 minutes longer, until the omelet is lightly browned on the bottom. Transfer the skillet to the oven and broil, 6 inches from heat, until eggs are no longer runny, 1 to 2 minutes. Let rest for 5 minutes before slicing into 4 to 6 wedges. Season the tomatoes with salt, spoon on top of the omelet, and top with a dollop of yogurt.

Stir-Fried Greens and Basil

Bags of prewashed and trimmed leafy greens are a brilliant idea and make it even easier to eat great healthy vegetables like these.

Serves 4 to 6

2 tablespoons olive oil

$1/2$ teaspoon crushed red pepper

2 large shallots, thinly sliced (about $1/2$ cup)

4 garlic cloves, thinly sliced

1 pound chard or spinach greens, stalks and spines removed, torn into small pieces

$1^1/2$ pounds mustard or turnip greens, stalks and spines removed, torn into small pieces

3 cups loosely packed basil leaves

2 teaspoons fresh lemon juice (from about $1/4$ lemon)

Salt and freshly ground black pepper

In a large nonstick skillet or wok, heat the olive oil over medium heat. Stir-fry the pepper, shallots, and garlic for 1 minute (do not brown). Remove with a slotted spoon and transfer to a plate. Add the greens to the skillet in batches along with ¼ cup water (or chicken broth) and stir-fry until wilted, about 5 minutes. Cover with a lid and steam until just tender but still green, 8 to 10 minutes. Remove from the heat and toss with the basil, shallots, garlic, and the lemon juice until the basil wilts. Season with salt and pepper to taste.

QUICK SIMPLE IDEA

Wash the greens well in a sink of cold water and a dash of vinegar to remove any grit, and add the greens while still wet to the pot—this helps them steam. Serve with grilled sausages or place a mound of greens on a plate and arrange fish fillets (such as Teriyaki-Glazed Salmon, page 148) on top, sprinkling with toasted sesame seeds.

Grilled Tomato-Corn Salsa

Makes 3 cups

10 plum tomatoes (about 2 pounds)

2 to 3 jalapeño peppers

2 ears corn, shucked

2 garlic cloves, minced

¼ cup coarsely chopped fresh cilantro

1 tablespoon extra-virgin olive oil

1 tablespoon fresh lime juice (from about 1 lime)

Salt and freshly ground black pepper

Over hot coals (or medium-high heat on a gas grill), cook the tomatoes and jalapeños, turning frequently, until the skins are charred and lightly wrinkled, about 5 minutes. Grill the corn, turning frequently, until lightly charred on all sides, about 5 minutes. Set aside to cool. Peel the skins from the tomatoes and chop, seed the jalapeños and mince, and cut the kernels from the corn. In a bowl, combine with the garlic, cilantro, oil, and lime juice and toss. Add salt and pepper to taste.

QUICK SIMPLE IDEA

Charring the ingredients on the grill gives this salsa a great smoky flavor. If you're going to the trouble of lighting the grill, you will want some extra salsa; it keeps well in the fridge for 1 to 2 weeks. Serve with chips or as a sauce for huevos rancheros or grilled fish, steak, or chicken.

Roasted Eggplant Spread

Makes 1½ cups

1 medium eggplant (about 1½ pounds), halved lengthwise

3 teaspoons olive oil, for brushing

4 cloves garlic, unpeeled

1 tablespoon fresh lemon juice (from ½ lemon)

2 tablespoons tahini (sesame paste)

Salt and freshly ground black pepper to taste

Preheat the oven to 425°F.

Brush the eggplant with the oil, lay cut-side down on a large baking sheet, and prick a few holes in the skin. Brush the garlic cloves with oil and place on the sheet next to the eggplant. Bake for 25 to 30 minutes, until the eggplant is very soft. Let cool until it is warm enough to handle. Scoop out the pulp with a spoon (hold the eggplants with an oven mitt if still hot) and discard the skin. Place the pulp in a strainer and drain for 15 minutes. Squeeze the garlic flesh from the skins and mash with a fork. Combine the eggplant and garlic in a bowl and whisk to blend, beating it to make it creamy and relatively smooth. Whisk in the lemon juice and tahini and season to taste with salt and pepper. Serve warm or at room temperature.

QUICK SIMPLE IDEA

This is a smoky-flavored spread that's best served warm on heated pita wedges or flatbread crackers.

Grilled Mexican Corn

Serves 2 to 4

4 ears corn

Salt

2 tablespoons (¼ stick) salted butter, melted

4 ounces queso fresco (Mexican fresh cheese)
   or feta cheese

Cayenne

Lime wedges

Husk the corn and break off the stem end. Pull off as much silk as you can and briskly brush the remaining silk from the corn with a dry vegetable brush. Bring a large pot of water to a boil (it should cover the corn) and add salt. Cook the corn, uncovered, for 2 minutes; drain. Heat a grill to medium high. Grill the corn until the kernels are lightly charred, about 5 minutes. Transfer to a platter and brush quickly with the butter. Finely grate the cheese over the corn, sprinkle with cayenne to taste, and drizzle with a little lime.

Simple Mashed Potatoes

To make great mashed potatoes, all you need is a large pot and a sturdy potato masher. Here is a basic recipe plus a few tasty variations.

Serves 4 to 6

2 pounds russet or Yukon Gold potatoes, peeled and cut into 1-inch pieces

4 tablespoons (1/2 stick) unsalted butter, plus more to taste, at room temperature

1/2 to 2/3 cup whole milk or half-and-half, warmed

3/4 teaspoon salt, or more to taste

1/4 teaspoon freshly ground black pepper, or more to taste

Place the potatoes in a large pot with enough salted cold water to cover. Bring to a boil, reduce the heat to medium, partially cover, and cook for 10 to 15 minutes, until tender. Drain and return the pot of potatoes to the heat to dry, shaking, until a film forms on the bottom. Remove from the heat, add the butter, and mash, using just enough milk to make the potatoes creamy. Add the salt and pepper and serve hot, with a lump of butter on top.

Wasabi Mashed Potatoes

Boil the potatoes as directed in the basic recipe. Fold in 3 to 4 tablespoons wasabi paste (available in the Asian food section of the supermarket or in health food stores).

Basil Mashed Potatoes

Boil the potatoes as directed in the basic recipe. Mash with 2 tablespoons butter and fold in 2 to 4 tablespoons Simple Pesto (page 50). Drizzle with extra-virgin olive oil.

Garlic Mashed Potatoes with Peas

Sauté 3 minced garlic cloves in 4 tablespoons butter. Add to the cooked potatoes with 1/2 cup sour cream instead of the milk, and mash as directed. Fold in 1/2 cup petit frozen peas that have been thawed in warm water and drained. Top with more butter, if desired.

QUICK SIMPLE IDEA

For ultra-creamy whipped potatoes, beat them with an electric mixer until smooth. Peeling thin-skinned potatoes is optional; russet potatoes should be peeled before mashing. You can turn leftovers into a clever side dish the next day: Pile potatoes into a buttered dish and top with grated sharp white Cheddar and crumbled bacon; bake until hot and bubbly.

Salt-Baked Crushed Potatoes with Lentils and Fried Onions

Serves 4 to 6

1 cup dried brown or green lentils

1 bay leaf

1¼ cups coarse sea salt

6 to 8 medium Yukon Gold potatoes (about 2½ pounds), scrubbed and patted dry

2 tablespoons (¼ stick) unsalted butter

2 tablespoons plus 2 teaspoons extra-virgin olive oil, plus more for drizzling

Kosher salt and freshly ground black pepper to taste

1 medium onion, very thinly sliced

Preheat the oven to 425°F. In a large saucepan filled with 3 cups of boiling salted water, cook the lentils with the bay leaf until just tender, about 25 minutes (do not cook to mush). Drain and keep warm.

Meanwhile, spread the sea salt evenly over the bottom of a 9 × 13 × 2-inch baking dish. Place the potatoes on top of the salt and bake for 45 to 50 minutes, or until tender when pierced with a knife. Set the potatoes aside to cool for a few minutes; discard the salt. Peel the potatoes while still warm (use oven mitts) or leave the skins on. Place the potatoes in a metal bowl with the butter, 2 tablespoons of the olive oil, and salt and pepper. Crush or mash the potatoes with a fork or masher (they should be chunky); cover with foil and keep warm. In a nonstick skillet over a medium-high flame, heat the remaining 2 teaspoons of oil. Fry the onion until browned and crispy, about 5 minutes, then remove from the heat. Spoon the lentils on top of the potatoes, drizzle with a little olive oil, and sprinkle with salt and pepper. Top with the onion and serve hot.

QUICK SIMPLE IDEA

These mashed potatoes are special—thick and chunky, they taste purely of potato—and make a good base for steak or fish fillets, especially drizzled with lemon- or basil-flavored olive oil. They take a little longer to bake, so put them in the oven before you make the rest of your meal.

Oven Frites

A dark, nonstick, or well-used baking sheet with a good patina makes the crispiest oven fries.

Serves 4 to 6

5 medium russet potatoes (about 2 to 2$^1/_2$ pounds)

2 tablespoons olive oil, plus more for brushing

1 teaspoon kosher salt, plus more to taste

$^1/_4$ teaspoon freshly ground black pepper

Scrub the potatoes and cut them lengthwise into long, $^1/_2$-inch-thick fries. Soak in cold water for 20 to 30 minutes.

Preheat the oven to 425°F.

Drain the potatoes and wipe away most of the moisture with paper towels. Place the potatoes in a large bowl and toss them with the olive oil, salt, and pepper. Place 2 baking sheets in the middle of the oven. When the baking sheets are hot (after about 15 minutes), remove from the oven and lightly brush with olive oil. Arrange the potatoes in a single layer on the hot baking sheets with a little space in between. Return to the oven and bake until the potatoes are golden brown on the bottom, 15 to 20 minutes. Remove from the oven and turn with a wide spatula. Continue roasting until the fries are golden brown, 10 to 15 minutes longer. Sprinkle with more salt, if desired, and serve hot.

Sweet Potato–Chipotle Pancakes

Serves 4, makes 15 to 20 three-inch pancakes

$^3/_4$ cup all-purpose flour

1 teaspoon salt

1$^1/_2$ teaspoons ancho chili powder

1 large egg, beaten

2 teaspoons mild molasses or honey

1 pound sweet potatoes, peeled

3 canned chipotle peppers

Peanut oil for frying

In a medium bowl, whisk together the flour, salt, and chili powder. In the bowl of a food processor, purée the egg, molasses, and peppers. Pour the liquid ingredients over the dry ingredients and mix with a whisk until everything is just combined. Grate the sweet potatoes using the processor attachment (or the large holes of a box grater).

Cover the bottom of a large skillet with enough oil for a $^1/_4$-depth and place over medium heat. (Oil should be hot but not smoking.) Spoon about 2 tablespoons batter onto the skillet and spread it out to make a flat 3-inch pancake. (Do not crowd the skillet.) When the bottoms are golden brown, flip the pancakes over with a spatula and cook until the other sides are light brown, 1 to 2 minutes. Repeat with the remaining batter. Serve with Tamarind-Glazed Pork Tenderloins (page 133), or with sour cream.

Baked Sweet Potatoes

Freshly harvested sweet potatoes from the local farmer's market are the ultimate potato experience. I like placing them on the bottom rack so they get slightly charred an caramelized. You can cut the baking time in half by precooking the potatoes partially in the microwave.

Serves 6

6 medium sweet potatoes (4 to 5 pounds)

3 tablespoons unsalted butter, melted

Kosher salt to taste

2 tablespoons dark brown sugar

$3/4$ cup thick Greek-style whole milk yogurt or sour cream

Hot paprika or cayenne to taste (optional)

Preheat the oven to 425°F. and arrange the rack on the lowest rung.

Precook the potatoes in the microwave (three at a time) for 3 to 4 minutes. Place the potatoes directly on the bottom oven rack and bake until easily pierced with a knife, 20 to 30 minutes (some ovens cook hotter than others, so check at 15 minutes), turning a couple of times with oven mitts.

Break the potatoes open, drizzle with butter, and sprinkle with salt, if desired. Top with a little brown sugar, a dollop of yogurt or sour cream, and paprika or cayenne, if using. Serve piping hot

Spaghetti with Roast Tomato Sauce

Panfried Cabbage Noodles

Spicy Cinnamon Beef with Udon

Linguine with Walnuts and Arugula

Ziti with Garlic-Roasted Cauliflower

Farfalle with Zucchini and Lemon-Cream Sauce

Mac and Cheese with Sage Crumbs

Cellophane Noodles with Shiitake Mushrooms

Penne, Ham, and Asparagus Frittata

Yellow Saffron Rice

Coconut Basmati Rice

Vegetable Fried Brown Rice

Giant Ravioli with Lamb Ragù

Lamb Ragù

Spicy Black Beans

Roasted Corn and Barley Pilaf

Orecchiette with Spring Peas and Brown Butter

Quinoa-Edamame Pilaf

Couscous Tabbouleh

Ginger and Cardamom–Scented Jasmine Rice

Lemon-Chard Bulgur Risotto

Singapore Noodles

noodles, rice, grains

Whatever the season, a bowl of noodles or rice can be the beginning of endless satisfying meals. Buy imported Italian dried pasta (or use fresh pasta), really good fresh Asian noodles, or dried ones off the shelf. Combine them with leafy greens, tender vegetables fresh from the farmer's market, and shaved Parmesan over the top; no one will realize they're eating a vegetarian meal. Just boil water, dice, and toss. Use super convenient Asian curry pastes or sauces, add shellfish or stir-fried spicy cinnamon beef, and you're cooking global. Experiment with different grains, like quinoa, quick-cooking barley, buckwheat soba, and fragrant jasmine rice, to make traditional side dishes and meals in a whole new way. These are savory and hearty pleasures as good for you as they are good to eat.

Spaghetti with Roast Tomato Sauce

This is the easiest (and I think best) recipe for fresh tomato sauce, a great summer standby and perfect for spaghetti or any type of pasta. It's also good on grilled fish, vegetables, or polenta. You can make the sauce and keep it in the fridge for two or three days before you serve it.

Serves 4 to 6

4 garlic cloves, minced

1 cup finely chopped red onion (1 medium onion)

2 teaspoons chopped fresh thyme or 1 teaspoon dried

Pinch of crushed red pepper

4 tablespoons extra-virgin olive oil

4 ripe beefsteak tomatoes (about 2 pounds)

Salt and freshly ground black pepper

1 pound spaghetti, cooked al dente according to package directions, drained

Grated Parmesan cheese to taste

Preheat the oven to 450°F.

In a large baking pan (such as a lasagne pan), combine the garlic, onion, thyme, and red pepper. Drizzle with 3 tablespoons of the oil and stir to combine. With a sharp paring knife, remove the cone-shaped core on the top of each tomato, carve a shallow **X** in the bottom, and halve the tomatoes crosswise. Place the tomatoes, cut-side down, on top of the onion mixture. Roast for 25 to 30 minutes, until the tomato skins are blistered and wrinkled. Cool in the pan for 15 minutes, then pull the tomato skins off with your fingers. Transfer the pan's contents to a food processor or blender. Pulse 2 or 3 times to chop the tomatoes (do not purée). Season to taste with salt and pepper. Toss the sauce with the remaining tablespoon of oil, the hot cooked pasta, and Parmesan cheese.

Panfried Cabbage Noodles

Serves 4 to 6

2 tablespoons (¼ stick) unsalted butter

1 tablespoon olive oil

2 to 3 garlic cloves, minced

½ cup thinly sliced onion (½ medium onion)

12 Brussels sprouts, trimmed and thinly sliced (about ¼ pound)

1 pound Savoy or Napa cabbage, thinly sliced

1 tablespoon slivered fresh sage leaves (about 4 to 6) or minced rosemary leaves

Salt and freshly ground black pepper

8 ounces whole wheat (or regular) angel hair pasta

⅓ to ½ cup grated Asiago or Pecorino cheese

In a large nonstick skillet or wok over a medium flame, heat the butter and oil until they begin to brown. Add the garlic, onion, and Brussels sprouts and stir-fry for 1 minute. Add 1 tablespoon of water and stir-fry until the sprouts begin to soften, 3 to 5 minutes. Add the cabbage and continue stirring until it's cooked and a little browned, 1 to 2 minutes. Add the sage and season with salt and pepper to taste. Transfer to a large bowl and set aside.

Cook the pasta in a large pot of boiling salted water until just tender, about 5 minutes. Reserve 3 tablespoons of the pasta cooking water; drain the pasta, and add it to the bowl with the cabbage. Toss with the cheese, adding a little of the cooking water to make it creamy. Taste and add more salt and pepper, if desired. Return the skillet to medium-high heat. Add the pasta to the skillet, and cook for about 1 minute, until it begins to brown and turn crispy. Turn and brown another minute, or longer, depending on how crisp you like it. Serve hot with additional grated cheese.

Spicy Cinnamon Beef with Udon

Serves 4 to 6

1 serrano chili, thinly sliced with seeds

2 tablespoons low-sodium soy sauce

2 teaspoons grated fresh ginger

$3/4$ teaspoon ground cinnamon

2 tablespoons chopped fresh basil, plus 10 large whole leaves

1-pound boneless strip or sirloin steak, sliced crosswise into $1/3$-inch pieces

8 ounces fresh udon noodles (substitute Chinese lo mein noodles, or in a pinch, fettuccine)

1 tablespoon vegetable oil

$1/2$ cup thinly sliced red onion (about 1 small onion)

4 garlic cloves, thinly sliced

2 tablespoons hoisin sauce mixed with 2 tablespoons water

6 cups loosely packed baby spinach leaves (about 5 ounces), stemmed

Salt and freshly ground black pepper

2 scallions (white and green parts), thinly sliced

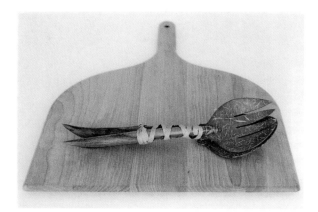

In a medium bowl, stir together the chili, soy sauce, ginger, cinnamon, and chopped basil, and toss with the beef. Marinate for 20 minutes at room temperature (or longer in the refrigerator). Just before you're ready to cook the beef, cook the noodles in a large pot of boiling water until tender, about 3 minutes (or longer if using dried noodles). Rinse in a colander under warm running water, drain, and set aside.

In a large nonstick skillet or wok, heat the oil over a medium-high flame. Add the onion and stir-fry for 1 minute, until soft. Add the beef, marinade, and garlic and stir-fry for 1 to 2 minutes, until the beef is seared but not well done. Add the hoisin sauce, spinach, and whole basil leaves and cook, stirring, until the spinach just wilts, about 1 minute. Season to taste with salt and pepper, remove from the heat, and sprinkle with the scallions. Serve hot over the noodles.

Linguine with Walnuts and Arugula

You can also stir-fry 12 or so peeled and deveined shrimp with the garlic and pepper flakes to make this simple dish even better.

Serves 4 to 6

3/4 cup marinated sun-dried tomato halves, drained and coarsely chopped

4 tablespoons olive oil

6 garlic cloves, thinly sliced

1/4 teaspoon crushed red pepper

10 cups loosely packed arugula or baby spinach leaves, stems discarded

1 tablespoon fresh lemon juice (from about 1/2 lemon)

3/4 pound linguine

Salt and freshly ground black pepper

1/3 cup freshly grated Parmesan or Pecorino cheese, plus more for serving

1 cup coarsely chopped toasted walnuts

Place the tomatoes in a small bowl with 1/2 cup of boiling water. Set aside. In a large skillet, heat the oil over a medium flame. Add the garlic and red pepper flakes and sauté for 30 seconds. Remove from the heat. Drain the tomatoes and add to the skillet along with the arugula and lemon juice, and toss to coat. Cook the pasta until al dente, about 3 minutes (or longer if using dried). Reserve 1/4 cup of the hot pasta water. Drain the pasta and add to the skillet with the arugula mixture, salt and pepper to taste, and the Parmesan cheese. Toss with just enough of the pasta water to make it creamy. Top with the walnuts and serve additional Parmesan on the side.

Ziti with Garlic-Roasted Cauliflower

Serves 4 to 6

One 2-pound head cauliflower, cut into florets

3 tablespoons plus 1 teaspoon extra-virgin olive oil

4 garlic cloves, coarsely chopped

2 tablespoons minced fresh rosemary leaves

1/2 teaspoon salt, plus more to taste

1/4 teaspoon freshly ground black pepper, plus more to taste

1 pound whole wheat (or regular) ziti, cooked al dente according to package directions, drained

1/2 cup pitted and halved kalamata olives (optional)

1/4 to 1/3 cup freshly grated Parmesan cheese

1/4 cup minced flat-leaf parsley

Preheat the oven to 425°F.

In a large bowl, toss the cauliflower with 3 tablespoons of the oil, the garlic, rosemary, salt, and pepper. Spread evenly in a shallow baking pan and roast, stirring occasionally, until golden and slightly charred, 25 to 30 minutes. Toss the hot pasta with the roasted cauliflower, the remaining teaspoon of olive oil, the olives, Parmesan cheese, parsley, and salt and pepper to taste.

QUICK SIMPLE IDEA

The garlic-roasted cauliflower makes a great side dish for a dinner buffet.

Farfalle with Zucchini and Lemon-Cream Sauce

Serves 4 to 6

6 garlic cloves, thinly sliced

2 tablespoons extra-virgin olive oil

3 small zucchini, ends trimmed and thinly sliced

Salt and freshly ground black pepper to taste

12 fresh basil leaves, slivered (about 1/4 cup)

Finely grated zest from 2 lemons

1/3 cup grated Parmesan cheese, plus more to taste

3/4 pound fresh or whole-milk ricotta, at room temperature

4 ounces mascarpone cheese, at room temperature

1 pound farfalle (bow-tie) pasta, cooked al dente according to package directions, drained

In a medium sauté pan, sauté the garlic in the oil over medium heat until fragrant, about 30 seconds. Add the zucchini and sauté for 1 to 2 minutes, until just tender; season with salt and pepper. In a medium bowl, stir together the basil, zest, Parmesan, ricotta, and mascarpone. Toss the drained pasta with the zucchini and cheese mixtures and season with salt and pepper to taste. Serve with additional Parmesan cheese.

Mac and Cheese with Sage Crumbs

The herb-crumb topping is optional but makes this into something special.

Serves 8 to 10

Basic White Sauce (recipe follows)

1½ teaspoons powdered mustard

¼ teaspoon cayenne

1 teaspoon salt

4 cups shredded extra-sharp white Cheddar cheese (about 16 ounces)

1 cup American cheese, broken into pieces (about 6 slices)

1 pound large macaroni, cooked according to package directions until al dente, drained

3 tablespoons unsalted butter

2 cups fresh bread crumbs

2 tablespoons finely chopped fresh sage or rosemary leaves

Preheat the oven to 350°F. Butter a 4-quart baking dish or casserole.

Make the white sauce in a large pot, remove from the heat, and stir in the mustard, cayenne, salt, cheeses, and the hot cooked macaroni. Transfer the mixture to the pre-pared dish. In a medium skillet over medium heat, melt the butter. Add the bread crumbs and sage and cook, stirring, until the crumbs begin to brown, 1 to 2 minutes. Scatter the crumbs over the macaroni mixture and bake for 25 to 30 minutes, until hot and bubbly and lightly browned.

Basic White Sauce
Makes about 4 cups

4 tablespoons (½ stick) unsalted butter

¼ cup plus 1 tablespoon all-purpose flour

4 cups whole milk

1 teaspoon salt

¼ teaspoon freshly ground white pepper

In a medium saucepan over medium heat, melt the butter. Whisk in the flour. Slowly add the milk in a steady stream, whisking to combine. Bring to a boil; reduce the heat to low and simmer until thickened, about 2 minutes. Season with the salt and pepper.

Cellophane Noodles with Shiitake Mushrooms

Cold leftover cellophane noodles are even better to have for lunch the following day.

Serves 4 to 6

6 ounces bean thread (cellophane) noodles

3 tablespoons light soy sauce

1 tablespoon sherry

2 tablespoons seasoned rice wine vinegar

1 teaspoon sugar

$1/4$ teaspoon Asian chili-garlic paste or crushed red pepper

1 tablespoon canola or safflower oil

$1/2$-inch piece fresh gingerroot, peeled and julienned

$1/2$ cup thinly sliced red onion (about 1 small onion)

8 ounces ($1/2$ pound) fresh shiitake mushrooms, stems discarded and caps thinly sliced

$1/2$ cup julienned or shredded carrot (about 2 medium carrots)

$1 1/2$ cups low-sodium canned chicken broth

4 scallions (white and light green parts), cut into 2-inch sections and julienned

In a medium bowl, soak the noodles in enough warm water to cover for 15 minutes. Drain and cut into 4-inch lengths. In a small bowl, stir together the soy sauce, sherry, vinegar, sugar, and chili paste and set aside.

In a large heavy saucepan or wok, heat the oil over a medium-high flame. Add the ginger, onion, mushrooms, and carrot and cook, stirring, for about 1 minute. Add a few tablespoons of the broth and continue stir-frying until the mushrooms are tender and the vegetables are limp, 1 to 2 minutes. Add the remaining broth, noodles, and scallions. Lower the heat to a simmer and cook, stirring occasionally, until the liquid is absorbed, 5 to 10 minutes. Drizzle the reserved sauce over the top, toss, and serve.

Penne, Ham, and Asparagus Frittata

Serves 6

1¹/₂ pounds thin asparagus

8 large eggs

¹/₄ teaspoon salt

Large pinch of freshly ground black pepper

1 tablespoon olive oil

1 tablespoon unsalted butter

1 extra-large onion, thinly sliced

2 cups cooked penne

¹/₂ cup diced cooked ham

2 teaspoons minced fresh rosemary leaves

¹/₂ cup freshly grated Parmesan cheese

Trim away all but 3 inches from the asparagus tips; discard the stems. Blanch the asparagus tips in boiling salted water until crisp-tender; drain under cold running water.

Preheat the oven to 425°F.

In a large bowl, beat the eggs with a fork and season with salt and pepper. In a 9- or 10-inch heavy-bottomed (or cast-iron) skillet, heat the oil and butter over a medium flame. Add the onion and cook, stirring, until soft, about 3 minutes. Reduce the heat to low and add the asparagus, penne, ham, and rosemary; toss to combine. Pour the eggs over the top. Cover the skillet and cook, without stirring, for 3 to 5 minutes, until the eggs are cooked around the edges.

Remove the lid and sprinkle with the Parmesan cheese. Transfer to the preheated oven and bake for 5 to 7 minutes, until just cooked through. For a brown crust, place the frittata under the broiler for 1 minute. Let stand for 5 minutes before slicing into six wedges.

Yellow Saffron Rice

Serves 4 to 6

2 cups Simple Chicken Stock (page 94) or low-sodium canned broth

Large pinch of saffron threads, crumbled (or 1/4 teaspoon ground saffron or turmeric)

1/2 teaspoon salt

2 cups long-grain white rice

1 tablespoon unsalted butter

Spicy Black Beans (page 83)

Place the broth, 2 cups of water, the saffron, and salt in a medium saucepan and bring to a boil. Add the rice and stir; reduce the heat to low, cover, and cook for 20 to 25 minutes, until the rice is tender. Let stand, covered, for 5 minutes, and stir in the butter before serving with Spicy Black Beans.

QUICK SIMPLE IDEA

Serve this with Asian-spiced dishes, such as the Swordfish Masala Kebabs with Mango Raita (page 152) or Ginger Chicken Satay with Grilled Mango (page 144). Top with minced cilantro leaves and cooked peas.

Coconut Basmati Rice

Serves 4 to 6

1 tablespoon unsalted butter, plus more to taste

1/2 cup finely chopped onion (about 1/2 medium onion)

1 1/2 cups basmati or other long-grain white rice

1 cup unsweetened light coconut milk, well stirred

1 teaspoon salt

1 teaspoon sugar

In a heavy, medium saucepan over medium heat, melt the butter. When foamy, add the onion and cook, stirring, until soft, about 2 minutes. Add the rice and stir to coat the grains, about 1 minute. Add the coconut milk, 1 1/4 cups water, the salt, and sugar. Stir well to combine. Bring to a boil and immediately reduce the heat to the lowest setting. Cover and cook for 25 minutes. Remove from the heat and let stand for 10 minutes. (The rice will stay hot for about 20 minutes left covered in the pan.) Add more butter, if desired, and fluff with a fork before serving.

Vegetable Fried Brown Rice

Serves 4 to 6

2 cups instant brown rice, cooked according to package directions (or regular brown rice)

1 tablespoon unsalted butter

4 large eggs, beaten

1 tablespoon canola oil

$1/2$ cup finely diced red or yellow onion (about $1/2$ medium onion)

$1/2$ cup frozen thawed peas and carrots

$1/2$ cup fresh or frozen thawed corn kernels

4 scallions (white and green parts), thinly sliced

1 medium tomato, seeded and chopped

Salt and freshly ground black pepper

$1/4$ cup finely minced fresh parsley or cilantro (optional)

Cook the rice and keep it warm. In a large nonstick skillet or seasoned wok over medium heat, melt the butter. Add the eggs and scramble until no longer runny. Transfer to a plate. Add the oil and onion to the skillet and stir-fry until soft, 2 to 3 minutes. Add the peas and carrots, corn, scallions, and tomato, and stir-fry for 1 minute. Add the cooked rice and reserved eggs and cook, stirring, until just heated through. Remove from the heat and season to taste with salt and pepper. Top with parsley or cilantro, if using.

QUICK SIMPLE IDEA

This is a good basic recipe for fried rice to which you can add your own favorite ingredients or leftovers such as thinly sliced chicken, shrimp, pork, or beef. Instant brown rice is a good substitute for the original—especially when you're in a hurry—as it takes only about 10 minutes from start to finish.

Giant Ravioli with Lamb Ragù

Fresh pasta sheets, sometimes called wrappers, can usually be found in the produce section with ethnic ingredients. They are delicate, so practice with a couple to get the hang of it.

Serves 4

1¼ cups fresh or whole milk ricotta

1 scallion (white and light green parts), finely chopped

2 tablespoons freshly grated Parmesan cheese, plus more to taste

1 teaspoon finely grated lemon zest (optional)

Salt and freshly ground black pepper

8 6-inch squares fresh pasta wrappers

Lamb Ragù (page 82)

In a small bowl, stir together the ricotta, scallion, Parmesan, zest (if using), and salt and pepper to taste. Bring a medium pot of water to a boil and add salt, then lower to a simmer. Place a damp tea towel on the counter and fill a medium bowl with cold water. Add 1 pasta sheet at a time to the simmering water and cook for 1 minute (but no longer), until pliable. Transfer the cooked pasta to the cold water with a slotted spoon for about 30 seconds, then spread it delicately on the tea towel. Repeat with the remaining pasta sheets.

Stir 2 tablespoons of the hot pasta water into the ricotta mixture. Place 4 pasta sheets in 4 shallow bowls. Spoon about ⅓ cup hot ragù on top, followed by a heaping tablespoon of ricotta, and another pasta sheet. Sprinkle with Parmesan cheese and a little pepper and serve.

Lamb Ragù

The sauce takes about 40 minutes to cook, but it can be made ahead and reheated; it can also be made with beef (or venison, if you can get it). The ragù makes a good basic meat sauce to toss with any pasta.

Makes about 4 cups

1¹/₂ pounds boneless lamb shoulder, trimmed and cut into 1/2-inch pieces

1 tablespoon olive oil

1 medium onion, finely chopped (about 1 cup)

3 garlic cloves, minced

4 ounces pancetta (or slab bacon), rind removed and diced

2 fresh bay leaves or 1 dried

2 tablespoons minced fresh marjoram or oregano (or 1¹/₂ teaspoons dried)

3 cups chopped vacuum-packed tomatoes (such as Pomi brand) with juice

2 tablespoons tomato paste

Place the lamb in the bowl of a food processor fitted with a metal blade and pulse to chop into fine pieces (but not enough to turn it into ground lamb). In a large nonstick skillet, heat the oil over a medium flame. Cook the onion, garlic, pancetta, bay leaves, and marjoram until soft and lightly browned—5 to 8 minutes. Raise the heat to medium high and add the lamb. Sear the lamb, stirring occasionally, until browned, 3 to 5 minutes. Add the tomatoes and tomato paste, reduce the heat to medium low, cover, and simmer, stirring occasionally, for 30 to 35 minutes (adding a little water as necessary), until the lamb is fork-tender. (The sauce should be brothy and not too thick.) Remove the bay leaves before serving.

Spicy Black Beans

Serves 4 to 6

2 tablespoons bacon drippings or olive oil

2 garlic cloves, minced

1 medium onion, diced

1 serrano or jalapeño chili, seeded and chopped

2 15-ounce cans black beans, rinsed and drained (or $1/2$ pound dried black beans, cooked according to package directions)

Salt and freshly ground black pepper

Yellow Saffron Rice (page 78)

In a large saucepan, heat the oil over a medium flame. Add the garlic, onion, and chili and sauté until the onion is soft, about 3 minutes. Add the beans and 3 tablespoons water and cook until heated through, 1 or 2 minutes. Season to taste with salt and pepper and serve with Yellow Saffron Rice.

Roasted Corn and Barley Pilaf

Serves 4

1 large ear corn, shucked

$3/4$ cup quick-cooking barley

2 plum tomatoes, seeded and diced

1 garlic clove, minced

$1/2$ jalapeño pepper, seeded and minced

2 tablespoons extra-virgin olive oil

1 tablespoon fresh lime juice (from 1 to 2 limes)

Salt and freshly ground black pepper

Preheat the oven to 450°F.

Place the corn on the center rack and roast, turning occasionally, until browned, 15 to 20 minutes. Meanwhile, bring the barley and 3 cups of salted water to a boil in a saucepan. Lower the heat and simmer for 10 minutes, drain, and cool under cold running water. Cut the corn kernels from the cob. In a large bowl, toss the corn, barley, and remaining ingredients together, Add salt and pepper to taste. Serve immediately or chill for 1 hour or overnight.

Orecchiette with Spring Peas and Brown Butter

Try this in the spring when English peas show up at the market. You may also serve it with grated Parmesan, if desired. Brown butter really makes the dish.

Serves 4 to 6

6 tablespoons (¾ stick) unsalted butter

1 pound orecchiette or medium shells

1 cup fresh peas or frozen thawed petit peas

2 Kirby cucumbers, peeled, seeded, and thinly sliced

1 cup shredded Boston or Bibb lettuce leaves

4 scallions, minced

¼ cup chopped fresh mint leaves

Salt and freshly ground black pepper

Place the butter in a small saucepan over medium heat. Skim the foam from the top and allow the butter to brown. Set aside to cool. Pour off the brown clarified butter from the top and discard the solids. Set aside.

Cook the pasta in a large pot of boiling salted water until nearly al dente. Add the peas and boil for 1 minute; drain. Meanwhile, place the cucumbers, lettuce, scallions, and mint in a large bowl. Add the hot pasta and the browned butter and toss with the vegetables. Season with salt and pepper to taste.

Quinoa-Edamame Pilaf

Quinoa is a great little grain that can be used much the same way as couscous in soups and salads, or as a side dish like rice. It's high in protein, light, and quite tasty, with a nutty undertone. It's available in supermarkets and health-food stores.

Serves 4

1 cup quinoa

1/3 cup thinly sliced scallion

1/2 cup frozen soybeans (edamame) or baby lima beans, blanched

Large pinch of kosher salt or fleur de sel

1 tablespoon fresh lemon juice (from about 1/2 lemon)

1 teaspoon extra-virgin olive oil

Rinse the quinoa well with water and drain in a fine-mesh sieve. Place the quinoa and 2 cups of cold water in a medium (1 1/2-quart) saucepan and bring to a boil. Reduce the heat to low, cover, and simmer until all the liquid is absorbed and the grain appears translucent, 12 to 15 minutes. Remove from the heat and allow to sit for 5 minutes. Fluff with a fork and toss in a bowl with the scallion, beans, salt, lemon juice, and olive oil.

Couscous Tabbouleh

Serves 6 to 8

1 cup dried couscous

1 cup chicken or vegetable broth

1 to 2 garlic cloves

1½ cups loosely packed fresh flat-leaf parsley

½ cup loosely packed fresh mint

1 Kirby cucumber, seeded and cut into ¼-inch dice (about 1 cup)

1 cup grape or cherry tomato halves

½ cup finely chopped scallion (white and green parts, about 4 scallions)

3 tablespoons extra-virgin olive oil

⅓ cup fresh lemon juice (from about 3 lemons)

Salt

Place the couscous in a medium metal bowl. In a small saucepan, combine the broth with ¼ cup of water and bring to a boil. Pour over the couscous, cover tightly with foil, and let stand for 5 minutes. Fluff with a fork and allow to cool. With the motor of a food processor running, drop in the garlic to mince. Add the parsley and mint and pulse until finely chopped. In another medium bowl, combine the cucumber, tomatoes, and scallion with the olive oil, lemon juice, and salt to taste. Let the mixture stand while the couscous cools. Pour the cucumber mixture over the couscous and stir in the parsley mixture. Toss well, cover, and chill for 30 minutes (or 1 day ahead). Fluff the salad before serving.

QUICK SIMPLE IDEA

You can use plain or whole-wheat couscous for this recipe. The salad can be made up to two days ahead of time, and the flavors only get better as they sit. It's a great side dish, but you can also add crumbled feta cheese and stuff it in pitas for a healthful sandwich.

Ginger and Cardamom–Scented Jasmine Rice

Serves 4 to 6

2 cups jasmine or other long-grain white rice

Pinch of cumin seeds

1 thin slice peeled fresh gingerroot

2-inch cinnamon stick

2 cardamom pods

1 fresh or dried bay leaf

In a heavy medium saucepan, place the rice, 2^1/$_4$ cups of water, and the spices and bring to a boil. Reduce the heat to its lowest setting, cover, and simmer for 15 minutes, until all the water is absorbed and the rice is tender. Remove from the heat and leave covered for 10 minutes to allow the rice to steam. Fluff with a fork and remove the ginger, cinnamon, cardamom, and bay leaf before serving hot.

Lemon-Chard Bulgur Risotto

Bulgur is a great substitute for rice in risotto without all that stirring. It is creamy, like grits, with a light wheat flavor.

Serves 4 to 6

2 tablespoons (1/4 stick) unsalted butter

1/2 medium onion, finely chopped (about 3/4 cup)

1 garlic clove, minced

2 teaspoons minced fresh rosemary

1 cup fine untoasted bulgur (cracked wheat)

2 1/2 cups Simple Chicken Stock (page 94) or low-sodium canned broth

3 cups loosely packed shredded Swiss chard leaves, ribs removed

1 teaspoon finely grated lemon zest

2 teaspoons fresh lemon juice (from 1/4 lemon)

1/3 cup freshly grated Parmesan cheese, plus more to taste

Salt and freshly ground black pepper

In a 2- to 3-quart heavy saucepan over medium heat, melt 1 tablespoon of the butter. Add the onion, garlic, and rosemary; cover and sweat until soft, about 2 minutes. Add the bulgur, 2 cups of the stock, and 1 1/2 cups of water and bring to a boil. Reduce the heat to low, cover, and simmer for 20 to 25 minutes, until the bulgur is tender and creamy. (There should still be some broth in the bottom of the pan.)

Remove from the heat and stir in the remaining tablespoon of butter, the chard, zest, lemon juice, and Parmesan cheese. Beat vigorously with a wooden spoon to make it creamier, adding enough of the remaining stock if it seems too thick. Season to taste with salt and pepper before serving.

Singapore Noodles

I make these vibrant curried noodles all the time. The greens or protein may change depending on what's in the fridge. Feel free to make substitutions.

Serves 4 to 6

8 ounces thin Chinese egg noodles or vermicelli

$1/2$ cup Simple Chicken Stock (page 94) or low-sodium canned broth

3 tablespoons low-sodium soy sauce

1 teaspoon brown sugar

$1/4$ teaspoon freshly ground white or black pepper

1 tablespoon vegetable oil

1 large onion, thinly sliced lengthwise

2 garlic cloves, minced

1 tablespoon finely minced fresh gingerroot

$1/2$ red bell pepper, thinly sliced

1 bunch of baby bok choy (about 4 ounces), thinly sliced lengthwise (or 4 cups shredded Napa cabbage)

$1 1/2$ tablespoons Madras curry powder

3 ounces sliced cooked ham, cut into thin strips

$1/4$ pound medium peeled and deveined shrimp

4 scallions (white and green parts), julienned

Cook the noodles in a large pot of boiling water for about 3 minutes, until just tender. Rinse in a colander beneath warm water. Set aside. In a small bowl, stir together the chicken stock, soy sauce, sugar, and pepper and set aside.

Heat a wok or large heavy skillet over a medium-high flame and add the oil. Add the onion, garlic, and ginger and stir-fry for 1 minute, until fragrant. Add the bell pepper, bok choy, and curry powder and stir-fry for 3 to 4 minutes, until vegetables are just tender. Add the reserved sauce, ham, shrimp, scallions, and drained noodles and toss lightly for 2 to 3 minutes, or until shrimp are pink and cooked through. Transfer to a platter and serve immediately.

Simple Chicken Stock
VEGETABLE STOCK

Classic Chicken Noodle Soup

Parsnip-Potato Soup

Hot-and-Sour Shrimp Soup

Cream of Tomato Soup

Fresh Tomato Soup

Root Vegetable Soup

Curried Tomatoes and Tofu

Butternut Squash–Apple Soup

French Onion Soup

Miso Soup with Udon, Shiitakes, and Bok Choy

Chinese Chicken Noodle Soup

Lentil-Rice Soup

White Bean–Escarole Soup with Polenta Croutons

Vegetarian Chili with Grilled Polenta

Grilled Polenta Rounds

Sancocho (Chicken, Sweet Potato,
and Hominy Soup)

Lamb Tagine

Stewed Lentils with Chorizo and Queso Fresco

Simple Fish Stew

soups
and
stews

**A pot of chicken noodle soup sim-
mering on the stove** says "home" like
nothing else. And a good soup starts with good
stock. Although you can get fairly good broth
in cartons and cans (in general, the brands in
health-food stores have less sodium and better
flavor), homemade is superior. If you don't have
the time or inclination to make stock, choose a
low-sodium canned or vacuum-packed broth.

Almost all the soups and stews here freeze
well and become even more flavorful the following day. All cook fairly quickly and don't
require a lot of stirring or focused attention.
Invest in a large, heavy soup pot with a tight-
fitting lid and a nice ladle that will lean on the
pot and not fall in the soup.

Simple Chicken Stock

Makes about 8 cups

2 pounds chicken backs and wings (plus any
   saved chicken carcasses)

1 large onion, quartered

2 large carrots, sliced

1 or 2 garlic cloves, peeled and smashed

1 celery stalk with leaves, chopped

1 bay leaf

4 parsley sprigs

1/4 teaspoon black peppercorns

Place all the ingredients and 10 cups of water in a large stockpot and bring to a boil. Reduce the heat to low and simmer for at least 45 minutes (or up to 2 hours), skimming foam and fat occasionally from the surface. Strain the stock through a damp double layer of cheesecloth into a large metal bowl and discard the solids. Fill a clean kitchen sink halfway with cold water and add ice to make an ice bath. Lower the metal bowl in the ice water and let cool to room temperature. Transfer to airtight storage containers and refrigerate or freeze until ready to use.

VARIATION: VEGETABLE STOCK

Leave out the chicken, double the amount of vegetables and parsley, and add 2 medium tomatoes, quartered; 1 thyme sprig; a 2-inch strip of lemon zest; and 2 or 3 tablespoons of dried mushrooms, washed to remove any grit. Strain, cool, and store as above.

QUICK SIMPLE IDEA

To make a really good stock, save roast chicken bones in the freezer. Put them in your biggest stockpot along with chicken necks, backs, and wings, vegetables, and seasonings. Make it on the weekend, when you have more time, and freeze the stock in airtight plastic containers.

Classic Chicken Noodle Soup

Serves 6 to 8

6 cups Simple Chicken Stock (at left) or
  low-sodium canned broth

4 chicken breasts (bones in)

1 bay leaf

2 large carrots, thinly sliced

1 large onion, thinly sliced

2 celery stalks, thinly sliced

3 tablespoons chopped flat-leaf parsley

1 tablespoon minced fresh dill

8-ounce package medium egg noodles

Salt and freshly ground black pepper

Place the stock, chicken, bay leaf, and 3 cups of water in a large deep pot and bring to a boil. Reduce the heat to low and simmer for about 30 minutes, until the chicken is cooked through. Transfer the chicken to a plate to cool. Strain the stock, discard the bay leaf, and skim off any fat. Return to the pot and bring to a boil. Add the carrots, onion, and celery. Reduce the heat to low and simmer until the vegetables are tender, 15 to 20 minutes, skimming occasionally.

Meanwhile, remove the skin from the chicken and debone; discard the skin and bones. Shred the meat. Add the chicken to the pot with the parsley, dill, and noodles. Bring to a steady simmer and cook until the noodles are just tender, about 10 minutes. Season to taste with salt and pepper.

Parsnip-Potato Soup

Parsnips have an interesting character—similar to carrots in their sweetness, yet with a wild, earthy flavor that tastes as if they just came from the garden.

Serves 6

2 medium boiling potatoes, peeled and diced

3/4 pound parsnips, peeled and finely chopped

1 small fennel bulb, chopped (about 1 cup)

1 medium onion, chopped

2 teaspoons minced fresh thyme

2 tablespoons (1/4 stick) unsalted butter

2 1/2 cups Simple Chicken Stock (preceding page)
  or low-sodium canned broth

1/3 cup apple cider or juice

1/4 cup heavy cream

Salt and freshly ground white pepper

In a large heavy pot, cook the potato, parsnips, fennel, onion, and thyme in the butter over medium heat, stirring, until the onion is soft, about 5 minutes. Add the stock and 2 cups of water and simmer, covered, for 20 minutes, or until the vegetables are very soft. In a blender, purée the soup in batches and return to the pot. Stir in the cider or juice, cream, and salt and pepper to taste. Cook over medium heat, stirring occasionally, until heated through (if the soup is too thick, add a little more water or stock). Ladle into soup bowls and serve hot.

Hot-and-Sour Shrimp Soup

Serves 2 to 4

2 ounces rice stick noodles

1 fresh lemongrass stalk

2 teaspoons vegetable oil

1 tablespoon minced shallot

1 jalapeño or serrano chili, seeded and minced

6 button mushrooms, thinly sliced

3 cups Simple Chicken Stock (page 94) or
   low-sodium canned broth

1 teaspoon sugar

Freshly ground white pepper

1 plum tomato, seeded and cut into strips

12 medium shrimp, peeled and halved
   lengthwise (about ¼ pound)

2 teaspoons low-sodium soy sauce

2 tablespoons fresh lime juice (from 2 to
   3 limes)

¾ cup bean sprouts

¼ cup fresh cilantro leaves

Place the rice noodles in a large bowl and cover with very hot (but not boiling) water. Soak for 10 minutes and rinse in a colander under cool water. Divide the noodles between 2 deep salad bowls.

Cut off the root end and top half of the lemongrass stalk. Cut in 2 pieces and smash with a mallet. Heat the oil in a saucepan over a medium flame. Stir-fry the lemongrass, shallot, chili, and mushrooms for about 1 minute. Add the stock, sugar, and pepper to taste. Reduce the heat to low and simmer for 3 minutes. Add the tomato, shrimp, soy sauce, and lime juice; simmer for 1 minute, until the shrimp turn pink. Ladle into the bowls over the noodles, top with the sprouts and cilantro, and serve.

QUICK SIMPLE IDEA

You can find fresh lemongrass in Asian food stores or some specialty produce markets. The rice stick noodles are available in the ethnic food section of most large supermarkets. Fresh bean sprouts are usually in the refrigerated case of the produce section.

Cream of Tomato Soup

Serves 6 to 8

3 tablespoons unsalted butter

1/2 cup finely chopped onion (about 1/2 medium onion)

2 garlic cloves, minced

1 celery stalk, peeled and diced

1 medium carrot, grated

4 cups Simple Chicken Stock (page 94), Vegetable Stock (page 94), or low-sodium canned broth

1 teaspoon sugar

4 parsley sprigs

Two 26 1/2-ounce cartons vacuum-packed chopped tomatoes (such as Pomi brand), or 2 28-ounce cans crushed tomatoes

3/4 cup half-and-half

Salt and freshly ground black pepper

Melt 2 tablespoons of the butter in a soup pot. Add the onion, garlic, celery, and carrot and cook over medium heat, stirring, until the vegetables are softened but not browned, about 3 minutes. Add the stock, sugar, parsley, and tomatoes and bring just to a simmer. Simmer for about 30 minutes, or until the soup begins to thicken.

Process the soup in batches in a blender or processor (or use an immersion blender) to purée until smooth. Return to the pot and bring to a simmer. Stir in the half-and-half and the remaining tablespoon of butter, and season to taste with salt and pepper.

Fresh Tomato Soup

Serves 4

1 garlic clove

2 pounds ripe tomatoes, seeded and chopped (about 6 cups)

1/4 cup chopped fresh cilantro, plus additional for garnish

Salt and freshly ground black pepper

1/2 Hass avocado, diced and tossed with a little lime juice

1/4 cup plain whole-milk yogurt or sour cream (optional)

1 lime, quartered

1 teaspoon extra-virgin olive oil

With the motor of a blender or food processor running, drop the garlic through the chute and finely chop. Turn off the motor. Add the tomatoes and cilantro and pulse until the tomatoes are just puréed. Season to taste with salt and pepper. (The soup can be prepared to this point and chilled until ready to serve.) Pour into 4 bowls and top each serving with 1 tablespoon each diced avocado and yogurt and a squirt of lime. Drizzle lightly with a few drops of olive oil and garnish with cilantro.

QUICK SIMPLE IDEA

This is a cold soup that takes advantage of sweet, ripe, summer tomatoes. Look for tomatoes that are just soft to the touch and have a distinct fragrance. For a dinner party, top the soup with a few pieces of peeled cooked shrimp.

Root Vegetable Soup

Serves 6 to 8

1 tablespoon olive oil, plus more to taste

1 medium onion, chopped

2 garlic cloves, minced

1 small fennel bulb, trimmed and chopped (fronds reserved, chopped)

7 cups Simple Chicken Stock (page 94), Vegetable Stock (page 94), or low-sodium canned broth

2 cups cubed peeled butternut or acorn squash (about 1/2 pound)

1 1/2 cups cubed peeled rutabaga or turnips (about 1/2 pound)

2 medium carrots, sliced

2 cups thinly sliced fingerling potatoes (about 4 ounces)

2 thyme sprigs

10 Brussels sprouts, halved (about 1/4 pound), or 1 cup chopped cabbage

2 tablespoons minced flat-leaf parsley

1/2 teaspoon freshly grated nutmeg

Salt and freshly ground black pepper

Grated Parmesan cheese to taste

Heat the oil in a large deep pot over a medium flame. Sauté the onion, garlic, and fennel until soft, about 3 minutes. Add the stock, squash, rutabaga, carrots, potatoes, and thyme; if necessary, add enough water to cover the vegetables. Bring to a boil, reduce the heat to low, cover, and simmer for 20 to 30 minutes, until the vegetables are tender. Add the sprouts, parsley, and fennel fronds and simmer 10 minutes longer, until the sprouts are tender. Stir in the nutmeg and season to taste with salt and pepper. Top each serving with grated Parmesan and a few drops of olive oil, if desired.

QUICK SIMPLE IDEA

There is some chopping involved here, but this makes a big pot of soup to enjoy for several meals. You can also buy peeled and cut, ready-to-cook butternut squash, which will help speed things up. Serve it with cheese toasts or hot buttered corn bread.

Curried Tomatoes and Tofu

Serves 4

2 teaspoons olive oil

1 tablespoon finely grated fresh gingerroot

2 garlic cloves, minced

3^1/$_2$ cups firm tofu cubes (1 15-ounce package)

3 cups seeded and chopped tomatoes (4 to 5 medium tomatoes)

3 tablespoons chili sauce (such as Heinz)

1^1/$_2$ teaspoons sugar

2 teaspoons Madras curry powder

Salt and freshly ground black pepper

Heat the oil in a large nonstick skillet over a medium flame. Stir-fry the ginger and garlic until fragrant, about 30 seconds. Add the tofu, tomatoes, chili sauce, sugar, curry powder, and salt and pepper to taste. Stir-fry until slightly thickened and the tomatoes are soft and cooked, 3 to 5 minutes.

QUICK SIMPLE IDEA

This slightly tangy stew is best made with fresh tomatoes (you can use cherry tomatoes as well). Serve it with Yellow Saffron Rice (page 78) or couscous.

Butternut Squash–Apple Soup

Serves 4 to 6

2½-pound butternut squash

6 unpeeled garlic cloves

2 tablespoons unsalted butter

1 cup finely chopped onion (about 1 large onion)

1 large Granny Smith apple, peeled, cored, and chopped

1 teaspoon mace

Pinch cayenne

3½ cups Simple Chicken Stock (page 94) or low-sodium canned broth

¼ cup apple cider

Salt and freshly ground black pepper to taste

¼ cup heavy cream or whole-milk plain yogurt, room temperature (optional)

QUICK SIMPLE IDEA

Butternut squash does take some time in the oven to bake until soft, so I usually place it there the day before and refrigerate it until the next day. You can also garnish the soup with crisp bacon bits, or toast the seeds you remove from the squash, lightly salt, and scatter on top.

Preheat the oven to 425°F. Line a baking sheet with foil and lightly spray with oil.

Cut the squash in half lengthwise. Scoop out the seeds and discard (or remove the membranes and toast the seeds for garnish). Place the halves cut-side down on the baking sheet and place the garlic cloves under the halves. Bake for 35 to 40 minutes, until the flesh is soft and tender. Set the squash and garlic aside until cool enough to handle. (You can prepare the squash up to 2 days ahead.)

In a large (6-quart) saucepan, heat the butter over a medium flame. Sauté the onion, apple, mace, and cayenne for 5 to 7 minutes, until the onions and apple are very soft.

Scoop out the squash flesh with a spoon and place it in a food processor; discard the skin. Squeeze the garlic cloves from their skins into the processor; discard the skins. Add the apple and onions and purée until smooth and creamy. Return the purée to the saucepan and whisk in the chicken stock and cider. Bring to a boil, reduce the heat to low, and simmer for 5 minutes, until heated through (add more stock or water if the soup is too thick). Season to taste with salt and pepper. Ladle into bowls and swirl a little cream or yogurt over the top, if desired.

French Onion Soup

Serves 6 to 8

2 tablespoons olive oil

4 tablespoons unsalted butter

2 extra-large onions, thinly sliced

2 teaspoons sugar

3 cups Simple Chicken Stock (page 94) or low-
   sodium canned broth

3 cups low-sodium beef broth

1 teaspoon fresh thyme (or ½ teaspoon dried)

1 bay leaf

¼ cup dry red or white wine

Salt and freshly ground black pepper to taste

1 baguette, cut into 1-inch slices

½ cup grated Gruyère (2 ounces)

Heat the oil and 2 tablespoons of the butter in a large deep pot over a medium flame. Add the onions and sugar and stir to coat. Cover and cook, stirring occasionally, until the onions are limp but not completely tender, 5 to 8 minutes. Remove the lid and continue cooking, uncovered, until the onions are nicely browned. Add the stock and broth, thyme, and bay leaf and bring to a boil. Reduce the heat to low and simmer for 20 minutes. Add the wine and continue simmering, uncovered, for 5 minutes. Season with salt and pepper to taste.

Heat the broiler to high and place the rack 6 inches from the heat. Arrange the bread slices on a large baking sheet. Melt the remaining 2 tablespoons of butter in a small saucepan and brush the bread on both sides. Toast on both sides beneath the broiler, watching carefully.

Ladle the soup into ovenproof bowls, crocks, or ceramic coffee cups, and place them on a large baking sheet. Top with 1 or 2 slices of toast, and sprinkle with a small amount of Gruyère. Place the soup bowls beneath the broiler, watching carefully, to melt the cheese. Serve soups immediately.

QUICK SIMPLE IDEA

Instead of bowls, ladle this soup into large, heavy ceramic coffee cups, like those made for cappuccino. Top the soup with toasts and cheese and set the cups in their saucers to catch spills as you broil.

Miso Soup with Udon, Shiitakes, and Bok Choy

Serves 4

8 ounces fresh udon noodles (or dried udon)

6 cups Simple Chicken Stock (page 94), Vegetable Stock (page 94), or low-sodium canned broth

6 tablespoons yellow miso paste

4 ounces large shiitake mushroom caps (stems discarded), very thinly sliced (about 1 cup)

1 bunch of baby bok choy (about 4 ounces), very thinly sliced lengthwise

2 scallions (white and light green parts), thinly sliced

2 tablespoons low-sodium soy sauce

Cook the noodles in a large pot of boiling water until tender, about 3 minutes (or longer if using dried). Rinse in a colander beneath warm running water and set aside.

In a medium saucepan, bring the stock to a boil. Whisk in the miso and reduce to a simmer. Add the mushrooms and bok choy and cook until limp and tender, 1 to 2 minutes. Add the scallions, return to a simmer, and stir in the soy sauce. Remove from the heat. Divide the drained noodles among 4 bowls, pour the soup over the noodles, and serve.

QUICK SIMPLE IDEA

Miso is a highly flavorful vegetable paste made from fermented soy or grains like barley. You can add a teaspoonful to a vinaigrette or to enrich a sauce, but it is most frequently the start to a delicious and healthful soup. Miso can be found in the refrigerator section of the supermarket health-food department.

Chinese Chicken Noodle Soup

Serves 4 to 6

Two 3-ounce packages ramen noodles, broken into 3-inch lengths, seasoning discarded

2 teaspoons vegetable oil

3 teaspoons finely grated fresh ginger

3 garlic cloves, minced

6 cups Simple Chicken Stock (page 94) or low-sodium canned broth

2 boneless, skinless chicken breast halves, thinly sliced

1 tablespoon low-sodium soy sauce

Freshly ground white or black pepper to taste

4 cups thinly shredded Napa or Savoy cabbage (about ½ pound)

¾ cup diagonally sliced scallions (white and green parts)

1 cup loosely packed fresh cilantro leaves

Asian chili-garlic paste to taste (optional)

Place the noodles in a large bowl and cover with boiling water. Soak for 3 minutes. Drain and rinse beneath cold running water. Divide the noodles between 4 deep soup bowls. In a large saucepan, heat the oil over a medium flame. Add the ginger and garlic, and stir-fry for 1 minute. Add the stock, chicken, soy sauce, and pepper. Bring to a boil, reduce the heat to low, and simmer until the chicken is cooked, about 3 minutes. Remove from the heat and stir in the cabbage and scallions. Ladle the soup over the noodles, and top with cilantro leaves, and stir in chili-garlic paste to taste, if using.

QUICK SIMPLE IDEA

You can make this in one big bowl—just add the softened noodles to the soup pot. For a spicy soup, add a dash of chili-garlic paste.

Lentil-Rice Soup

Serves 4 to 6

4 cups Simple Chicken Stock (page 94), or low-sodium canned broth

1 cup brown lentils, picked over and rinsed

1 bay leaf

1¼ teaspoons salt

1 tablespoon olive oil, plus more for drizzling

1 cup chopped yellow onion (about 1 medium onion)

3 cloves garlic, minced

½ medium carrot, grated

2 teaspoons minced fresh rosemary or thyme, or 1 teaspoon dried thyme

1 teaspoon ground cumin

¾ teaspoon madras curry powder

¼ teaspoon cayenne

1 cup cooked white or brown rice

In a large pot, combine the stock, 2 cups of water, the lentils, bay leaf, and salt. Bring to a boil, reduce the heat to low, cover, and simmer 25 minutes, until the lentils are cooked, occasionally skimming off the foam.

Meanwhile, in a medium saucepan, heat the oil over a medium-high flame and sauté the onion, garlic, carrot, rosemary, cumin, curry, and cayenne. Cover and cook for 5 minutes, until the vegetables are soft. Remove from the heat. When the lentils are cooked, add the vegetables and cooked rice to the lentils and simmer for 5 minutes, skimming occasionally. Discard the bay leaf. Remove a quarter of the soup and pulse a few times in a blender or processor until thick, then return to the pot. (Or use an immersion blender and pulse a few times until the soup is thickened.) Taste and adjust the seasonings. Drizzle with a little olive oil before serving, if desired.

White Bean–Escarole Soup with Polenta Croutons

Serves 4 to 6

Half a 24-ounce package basil-flavored ready-made polenta, sliced into ⅓-inch thick rounds

½ cup grated Parmesan cheese

1 tablespoon extra-virgin olive oil, plus more for garnish

2 garlic cloves, minced

1 sprig fresh thyme

1 head (1 pound) escarole, chopped

6 cups Simple Chicken Stock (page 94) or low-sodium canned broth

1 tablespoon tomato paste

1 cup broccolini or broccoli florets, steamed tender

Two 15½-ounce cans white cannellini beans, rinsed and drained

⅓ cup coarsely chopped flat-leaf parsley

Salt and freshly ground black pepper to taste

Preheat the broiler to high and place the oven rack on the highest rung. Line a large baking sheet with foil and lightly coat with olive oil cooking spray. Arrange the polenta rounds on the sheet and lightly spray with the oil. Broil, watching closely, for 3 to 5 minutes, until the polenta begins to turn golden brown and crispy. Turn and sprinkle ¼ cup Parmesan cheese over top. Broil 3 to 5 minutes longer, until golden brown. Remove from the oven and set aside to cool on sheet.

Meanwhile, heat the oil in a large pot over a medium flame. Add the garlic, thyme, and escarole and cook, stirring, until the escarole is wilted, about 3 minutes. Add the stock and paste and bring to a boil. Add the broccolini, beans, and parsley; lower the heat and simmer for 5 minutes. Season to taste with salt and pepper.

Slice the polenta into 4 pieces. Ladle the soup into bowls and top with a few polenta croutons, a few drops of olive oil, and the remaining Parmesan.

QUICK SIMPLE IDEAS

The crunchy polenta croutons are good on virtually any kind of soup—even your favorite canned selection. The croutons make a nice snack or appetizer to serve at a dinner party.

Vegetarian Chili with Grilled Polenta

Serves 4

1 tablespoon olive oil

1 medium onion, finely chopped

2 garlic cloves, minced

2 tablespoons ancho chili powder

1$\frac{1}{2}$ teaspoons ground cumin

14$\frac{1}{2}$-ounce can diced tomatoes with juice

15$\frac{1}{2}$-ounce can red kidney beans, rinsed and drained

15$\frac{1}{2}$-ounce can chickpeas or cannelloni beans, rinsed and drained

8-ounce can vegetarian beans

1 tablespoon red wine vinegar

Salt and freshly ground black pepper

Grilled Polenta Rounds (recipe follows)

Toppings: grated cheese, diced onion, tomatoes, salsa (optional)

Heat the oil in a large skillet over a medium flame. Add the onion, garlic, chili powder, and cumin and sauté until the onion is soft, about 5 minutes. Add the tomatoes and 1 cup of water, and simmer, partially covered, for 10 minutes. Add the three types of beans, return to a simmer, and cook, uncovered, for 20 to 30 minutes, until the chili is thick. Remove from the heat, stir in the vinegar, and season to taste with salt and pepper. Ladle into shallow bowls and add 2 slices of grilled polenta to each. Top with the cheese and other condiments, if using.

QUICK SIMPLE IDEA

If you want to make the chili heartier (and non-vegetarian), sauté $\frac{1}{2}$ pound ground sirloin or turkey. Drain off the fat and add to the recipe.

Grilled Polenta Rounds

Serves 4

Olive oil cooking spray

Half a 24-ounce package precooked polenta, cut
    into 8 slices

Before lighting or heating your grill, spray
the grids with cooking oil. Heat to medium.
Spray the polenta rounds with oil and grill
on both sides until lightly browned and
heated through. Alternately, heat the broiler
to high and spray a large baking sheet with
oil. Arrange the polenta slices in the pan
and spray to lightly coat. With the sheet
set on the highest rung of the oven, broil
for 5 minutes per side, until browned and
heated.

QUICK SIMPLE IDEA

Precooked polenta comes in rolls in the refrigerator
case. All you do is slice it and grill or broil it until
hot and lightly browned; you can also brown it in a
lightly oiled nonstick skillet. Sprinkle with
Parmesan or other cheeses.

Sancocho

Chicken, Sweet Potato, and Hominy Soup

Sancocho is a South American soup or boiled dinner. This one has a coconut-based chicken soup and is aromatic with exotic flavors.

Serves 4 to 6

2 skinless, boneless chicken breast halves

4 cups Simple Chicken Stock (page 94) or low-sodium canned broth

1 medium yellow onion, diced

2 garlic cloves, minced

1 serrano or jalapeño chili, seeded and finely sliced

1/2 red bell pepper, thinly sliced

2 tablespoons olive oil

1 medium sweet potato, peeled, diced, and parboiled

15-ounce can white hominy, rinsed and drained

14-ounce can unsweetened canned coconut milk, well stirred

2 plum tomatoes, seeded and chopped

Salt and freshly ground white pepper

1/3 cup avocado slices tossed in 2 teaspoons lime juice

1 lime, quartered

2 tablespoons chopped fresh cilantro

Simmer the chicken in the stock and 2 cups of water for 15 to 20 minutes, or until the chicken is just cooked through. Transfer to a cutting board to cool and slice into large pieces; strain the broth and reserve.

Sauté the onion, garlic, chili, and bell pepper in the oil in a deep pot over medium heat. Cook, stirring, for 5 minutes, until tender. Add the stock and bring to a boil. Add the sweet potato and hominy. Simmer for 15 to 20 minutes, or until the sweet potato is tender. Add the reserved chicken, coconut milk, tomatoes, and salt and pepper to taste. Ladle into deep soup bowls and top with avocado, a squeeze of lime, and cilantro.

Lamb Tagine

Serves 4

1¹/₂ tablespoons vegetable oil

2¹/₂ pounds 1-inch-thick lamb shoulder chops, trimmed and cut into 1/2-inch pieces

1 large onion, chopped

¹/₂ teaspoon turmeric

¹/₂ teaspoon salt, plus more to taste

¹/₄ teaspoon freshly ground black pepper

1 long strip orange zest (1 × 2 inches)

2 medium carrots, sliced into ¹/₄-inch-thick pieces

1 small sweet potato, peeled and cut into ¹/₂-inch chunks

1 medium turnip, peeled and cut into ¹/₂-inch chunks

2-inch cinnamon stick (or 1 teaspoon ground cinnamon)

1 cup pitted prunes

Heat 1 tablespoon of the oil in a heavy-bottomed deep saucepan (preferably nonstick) with a tight-fitting lid over a medium-high flame. Add half of the meat, brown on both sides (about 2 minutes), and transfer to a plate. Brown the remaining meat, transfer to a plate, and set aside. Add the remaining ¹/₂ tablespoon of oil to the pan with the onion and cook, stirring, until the onion is soft, about 2 minutes. Return the meat to the pan with the turmeric, salt, pepper, orange zest, and 2 cups of water. Bring to a boil, stirring up the brown bits. Cover tightly, reduce the heat to low, and simmer until the lamb is tender, about 30 minutes. Add the carrots, sweet potato, turnip, cinnamon, and prunes, and more water if necessary. Cover and simmer for 5 to 10 minutes, until the vegetables are tender. Season with additional salt, pepper, and spices to taste. Remove the cinnamon stick before serving.

QUICK SIMPLE IDEA

The recipe takes a bit longer to put together and cook (45 minutes to 1 hour) than others, but it's definitely worth the additional minutes. To save time, have your butcher trim and cut the lamb chops into small pieces. Serve the tagine with couscous.

Stewed Lentils with Chorizo and Queso Fresco

Serves 4

4 large garlic cloves, minced

1 teaspoon ground coriander

$1/4$ teaspoon cayenne

1 tablespoon plus 2 teaspoons olive oil

4 cups Simple Chicken Stock (page 94), Vegetable Stock (page 94), or low-sodium canned broth

1 bay leaf

2 cups green or brown lentils, rinsed and picked over

8 small red- or yellow-skinned potatoes, quartered

$1/2$ pound chorizo, kielbasa, or other spicy cured sausage, diced

1 tablespoon fresh lemon juice (from about $1/2$ lemon)

1 small bunch arugula, tough stems removed

Salt and freshly ground black pepper

$1/2$ cup *queso fresco* (Mexican fresh cheese) or feta cheese, crumbled

In a deep saucepan, sauté the garlic, coriander, and cayenne in 2 teaspoons of oil for 30 seconds. Add the stock, bay leaf, and lentils and bring to a boil. Reduce the heat to low, cover, and simmer for 10 minutes. Add the potatoes, cover, and cook until the potatoes and lentils are tender but not mushy, about 15 minutes.

Meanwhile, brown the sausage in a nonstick skillet. When the stew is cooked, toss with the remaining tablespoon of oil, the lemon juice, arugula, and salt and pepper to taste. Transfer to bowls and top each serving with sausage and cheese.

QUICK SIMPLE IDEA

Lentils cook quickly and are very flavorful, so they're ideal for a fast dinner. For an all-vegetable stew, omit the sausage or substitute prepared smoked tofu or tempeh. I usually serve this dish hot, but it's also nice at room temperature or chilled as a salad: Drizzle it with a little lemon juice and toss in more arugula leaves, radishes, and scallions.

Simple Fish Stew

Ask your fishmonger to peel and devein the shrimp, but to provide you with the shells (and maybe a fish head or two) for the stock; making your own stock (the first step in the recipe) is optional, but the result is a far richer soup. Instead of bread, you could add cooked rice or thinly sliced potatoes to the stew—it's hard to mess up!

Serves 4

8 jumbo shrimp, peeled, deveined, and sliced in half lengthwise (shells reserved)

3 tablespoons olive oil, plus more for drizzling

1 small onion, finely chopped

1 small fennel bulb, finely chopped, fronds reserved

4 cloves garlic, 3 minced and 1 whole

1¼ cups dry white wine

1 pound assorted skinless white-fleshed fish fillets (such as sea bass, cod, snapper, or halibut), cut into large chunks

1 cup seeded and coarsely chopped ripe plum tomatoes (or use canned)

Salt and freshly ground black pepper to taste

4 slices crusty bread

Place the shrimp shells in a saucepan with 2 cups of cold water and bring to a boil. Simmer for 5 minutes and skim the foam; strain, and reserve.

Heat 2 tablespoons of the oil in a large saucepan over a medium flame. Add the onion, chopped fennel, and garlic and sauté until the vegetables are soft, about 3 minutes. Add the wine, bring to a boil, and reduce by half, about 3 minutes. Chop fronds to make ¼ cup. Add the fish fillets. Lower the heat, cover, and simmer for 3 minutes. Add the tomatoes, shrimp, reserved shrimp broth, and enough water to cover the stew ingredients by 1 inch. Simmer, uncovered, for 5 minutes, or until the fish is cooked through. Season to taste with salt and pepper. Add the fennel fronds and set aside.

Toast the bread slices. While still hot, lightly brush or drizzle them with the remaining tablespoon of oil. Cut the whole garlic clove in half and rub the bread slices until the clove is dissolved. Place the toasts in the bottom of 4 shallow soup bowls, ladle in the soup, and drizzle with a little oil before serving, if desired.

Cowboy Steaks with Pico de Gallo

Grilled London Broil with Green Olive Tapenade

Perfect Grilled Steak

Steak Asada Tacos with Simple Guacamole

Plantains with Picadillo

Rosemary-Wrapped Filet Mignon

Tarragon-Crusted Loin Chops

Honey-Grilled Pork Tenderloin with
Fresh Plum Chutney

Tamarind-Glazed Pork Tenderloins

Spicy Meat and Feta Pizza

Orange Beef and Broccoli Stir-fry

Coriander Lamb Racks with Blackberry Sauce

Tuscan Peppered Wings

Real Good Turkey Burgers

Turkish Meat Loaf

Herbed Grilled Chicken

Chicken with Lemon–Green Olive Sauce

Ginger Chicken Satay with Grilled Mango

Salt-and-Pepper Roast Cardamom Chicken

Teriyaki-Glazed Salmon
with Pickled Cucumber Relish

Curried Monkfish with Tomatoes and Chilies

Panko-Crusted Fish and Chips

Swordfish Masala Kebabs with Mango Raita

meat, chicken, fish

Shrimp and Scallop Ceviche

Sake-Marinated Tuna Steaks with Miso Vinaigrette

Roasted Whole Snapper on a Bed of Lemons

Sole with Tomato-Butter Sauce

Barbecued Salmon with Potatoes

Juniper-Steamed Lobster with Ginger Butter

Quick Simple Paella

Thai Curried Mussels with Coconut Broth

Skewered Shrimp with Duck Sauce

Succotash Sauté with Shrimp

Life is for living and steaks are for grilling. Whether red-blooded or cold-blooded, meat, poultry, and fish are what's for dinner. These recipes are all easy to cook, and many follow a formula: marinating or seasoning with spice before heading for the grill or sauté pan for a quick searing. All you need is a good, heavy skillet or grill pan, or a real grill. You can also use an indoor grilling appliance; just be sure to check the manufacturer's instructions for cooking times. A few recipes require roasting and a bit more time (but not too much attention). Almost all of them are speedy enough for a weeknight, but also special enough to share with friends. Reserve the few that measure longer on a stopwatch for special Saturday nights.

Cowboy Steaks with Pico de Gallo

These macho spiced steaks are ideal cooked over a charcoal fire. Barring that, they're still pretty good on a gas grill or panfried on your stovetop.

Serves 4

1½ tablespoons chili powder

½ teaspoon ground cumin

1 teaspoon cayenne

1 teaspoon garlic powder

1 tablespoon salt, plus more to taste

4 rib-eye steaks, 1 inch thick (about 14 ounces each)

2 large onions, sliced ¾ inch thick

Vegetable oil for brushing

Freshly ground black pepper to taste

Pico de Gallo (recipe follows)

Special equipment: Wooden skewers, soaked in water for 20 minutes

In a small bowl, stir together the chili powder, cumin, cayenne, garlic powder, and salt. Rub on both sides of each steak and set aside. Thread the onion slices on the well-soaked skewers, about 2 on each, so that the onions will lie flat on the grill. Brush with the vegetable oil and season with salt and pepper. Heat the grill to medium high. Arrange the onions and steaks on the grill. Cook the onions until tender, 6 to 8 minutes, and the steaks for 4 to 5 minutes per side for medium, or longer for the desired doneness. Let the steaks rest for 3 to 4 minutes, top with the onions, and serve with Pico de Gallo.

Pico de Gallo

Makes about 2½ cups

3 medium tomatoes, seeded and finely chopped

¼ cup chopped red onion (from about ½ small onion), rinsed in cold water

1 garlic clove, minced

2 tablespoons fresh lime juice (from 2 to 3 limes)

1 to 2 jalapeño peppers, seeded and minced

¼ cup chopped fresh cilantro leaves

Salt to taste

In a glass bowl, stir all the ingredients together and let sit for 15 minutes before serving.

Grilled London Broil with Green Olive Tapenade

Serves 6

4 garlic cloves

1 tablespoon crushed black peppercorns

3 teaspoons extra-virgin olive oil

2 tablespoons bourbon or Cognac

1½ pounds top round London broil (about 1¼ inches thick)

Green Olive Tapenade (recipe follows), optional

Place the garlic, peppercorns, oil, and bourbon in a blender or food processor and purée. Place the London broil in a large resealable plastic bag with the marinade. Seal the bag, pressing out any excess air, and put in a shallow baking dish. Marinate at room temperature for 30 minutes (or overnight in the refrigerator).

Lightly spray a clean grill with cooking oil and preheat to medium high (or over medium coals). Remove the steak from the marinade and let the excess marinade drip off. Grill for 7 to 9 minutes per side for medium-rare (or longer for medium). Transfer to a cutting board and let stand for 10 minutes, then cut across the grain into thin slices. Serve with a spoonful of tapenade.

Green Olive Tapenade

Makes about 1¼ cups

1 cup pitted green Sicilian olives

1 tablespoon drained capers

2 anchovy fillets, rinsed

½ teaspoon finely grated lemon zest

2 teaspoons fresh lemon juice (from about ¼ lemon)

¼ cup loosely packed flat-leaf parsley, stems removed

Freshly ground black pepper to taste

3 tablespoons extra-virgin olive oil

Place all the ingredients except the olive oil in a food processor and pulse a few times until the mixture is finely chopped but not quite puréed. Stir in the olive oil.

QUICK SIMPLE IDEA

You can also cook London broil under a hot broiler. The longer the meat marinates the more flavorful and tender it becomes—you can even prep it a day ahead. Serve with thick-sliced, super-ripe tomatoes and the tapenade.

Perfect Grilled Steak

Serves 4

3 tablespoons unsalted butter, melted

2 tablespoons olive oil

4 T-bone or New York strip steaks, about 1 inch thick (about 1 pound each)

Kosher salt to taste

Freshly ground black pepper to taste

Mix the butter and the oil on a plate and coat each steak on both sides. Sprinkle well on both sides with salt and pepper. Set the steaks aside to warm at room temperature for about 20 minutes.

To grill: Heat the grill or coals to medium high. Sear for 2 minutes, uncovered, and cook the other side for 2 minutes, uncovered. The steaks should take 4 to 5 minutes of cooking; a meat thermometer should read around 140°F. for medium. Cook more or less depending on the desired doneness.

To panfry: Lightly oil a heavy cast-iron or heavy ridged grill pan and place it over medium-high heat until very hot. Cook 1 steak at a time. Place the meat in the pan and cook, uncovered, for 2 minutes, then turn and cook 2 minutes longer for medium-rare. Reduce the heat slightly and cook 1 to 3 minutes longer, until it reaches the desired doneness.

QUICK SIMPLE IDEA

This is a basic recipe for grilling or panfrying steaks and thick chops of any type, including pork or veal. Before you heat your grill, make sure the grids are scraped clean and lightly oiled or coated with cooking spray to prevent the foods from sticking.

Steak Asada Tacos with Simple Guacamole

Serves 4 to 6

2 garlic cloves, minced

1/2 teaspoon cayenne

1 teaspoon dried Mexican oregano

4 teaspoons vegetable oil

Salt and freshly ground black pepper to taste

1 1/2 pounds flank or skirt steak

1 medium onion, thinly sliced

1 large red bell pepper, seeded and thinly sliced

2 jalapeño peppers, seeded and sliced into strips

Twelve 6- to 7-inch flour tortillas, warmed

Simple Guacamole (recipe follows)

Grilled Tomato-Corn Salsa (page 57), optional

In a small bowl, mix together the garlic, cayenne, oregano, 2 teaspoons of the oil, and the salt and pepper. Coat the steak on both sides and allow to rest for 20 minutes (or chill longer or overnight). Heat the grill to medium high, or set the broiler to high and arrange the oven rack closest to the heat. Cook the steak for 4 to 5 minutes per side for medium. Set aside and cover with foil for 5 minutes.

Heat the remaining 2 teaspoons of oil in a large nonstick skillet over medium-high heat. Add the onion, bell pepper, and jalapeños and cook until soft, about 5 minutes. Thinly slice the steak across the grain into strips. Serve with the onion mixture wrapped in the tortillas and the guacamole and salsa, if desired.

Simple Guacamole
Makes 1 1/2 cups

2 ripe Hass avocados

1 garlic clove, minced or pressed through a garlic press

2 teaspoons fresh lime juice (from about 1 lime)

Salt to taste

Peel and pit the avocados and mash with a fork. Add the garlic, lime juice, and salt.

QUICK SIMPLE IDEA

The longer the steak marinates, the more flavorful it is—and 2 days in the fridge would make it awesome. Sauté the onions and peppers while you broil or grill the meat, and have the tortillas warming in a covered casserole in a low oven. The soft tacos are good by themselves, or you can top them with guacamole and salsa.

Plantains with Picadillo

This is a great Latin-flavored skillet supper. Choose soft, ripe, black-skinned plantains.

Serves 4

1 tablespoon vegetable oil

1 medium onion, chopped

2 garlic cloves, minced

2 cups seeded and chopped plum tomatoes (about 6) or 1 (28-ounce) can tomatoes, drained and chopped

1 teaspoon ground cinnamon

¼ to ½ teaspoon cayenne

1 teaspoon dried marjoram

1 bay leaf

½ pound ground sirloin or pork

2 tablespoons golden raisins, soaked in warm water until soft, drained

2 very ripe black-skinned plantains

2 tablespoons unsalted butter

Salt and freshly ground black pepper to taste

⅓ cup sour cream mixed with 1 tablespoon milk

Heat the oil in a large nonstick skillet, over medium heat. Sauté the onion and garlic until the onion is limp, about 4 minutes. Add the tomatoes, cinnamon, cayenne, marjoram, and bay leaf and simmer, stirring, for 5 minutes. Add the meat, breaking up any clumps as it cooks. Stir in the drained raisins and cook until the meat is no longer pink, about 3 minutes. Remove the bay leaf; remove the pan from the heat, and keep warm.

Cut the ends from the plantains and peel them. Then cut in half crosswise, then again in half lengthwise to quarter them. Heat the butter in a large nonstick skillet over a medium flame. Sauté the plantains, turning occasionally, until they are nicely browned on all sides, 8 to 10 minutes. Transfer to a serving dish and season with salt and pepper to taste. Top with spoonfuls of the picadillo and drizzle with the sour cream mixture.

Rosemary-Wrapped Filet Mignon

Serves 4

2 tablespoons olive oil, plus more for oiling pan

2 tablespoons balsamic vinegar

1½ tablespoons coarse-grained mustard

1 teaspoon kosher salt

1 teaspoon freshly ground black pepper

6 to 8 long rosemary sprigs

4 6-ounce 1-inch-thick filet mignon steaks

Oven Frites (page 62), optional

Special equipment: Kitchen twine or string

In a large shallow bowl, mix together the oil, vinegar, mustard, salt, and pepper. Wrap a rosemary sprig around the edge of each steak and tie the ends securely with kitchen string. Repeat with the other steaks. Place the steaks in the marinade and turn to coat. Let sit at room temperature for 30 minutes (or longer, covered with plastic wrap and refrigerated).

If serving with the Oven Frites, make them and keep warm in a low oven while you cook the steaks. Lightly oil a heavy cast-iron or heavy ridged grill pan and place it over medium-high heat until very hot. Let the marinade drip off the filets, place the steaks in the pan, and cook, uncovered, for 2 minutes, then turn and cook 2 minutes longer for medium-rare. Reduce the heat slightly and cook 1 to 2 minutes longer, until they reach the desired doneness. Transfer to plates and serve with Oven Frites, if desired.

Tarragon-Crusted Loin Chops

Serves 4

1$\frac{1}{2}$ teaspoons hot paprika

1 fresh or dried bay leaf, crumbled

1 teaspoon plus a large pinch of kosher salt

$\frac{3}{4}$ teaspoon freshly ground black pepper

$\frac{1}{4}$ cup whole milk

2 tablespoons extra-virgin olive oil

4 1- to 1$\frac{1}{2}$-inch-thick pork or veal loin chops
   with bones, about 8 ounces each

1 cup coarse dry bread crumbs

$\frac{1}{4}$ cup toasted pine nuts or slivered almonds,
   coarsely ground

1 tablespoon minced fresh tarragon or
   2 teaspoons dried

Coarse-grained French Dijon mustard

Preheat the oven to 425°F.

Combine the paprika, bay leaf, 1 teaspoon salt, pepper, milk, and oil in a large shallow dish. Add the chops, turn to coat on both sides, and let sit at room temperature for 20 minutes (or longer in the fridge). Place the bread crumbs, pinch of salt, ground nuts, and tarragon on a plate and stir to combine. Coat each chop on both sides, pressing the crumbs in to make them adhere. Line a large baking sheet with foil and place a rack on top. Arrange the chops on the rack and bake for 20 to 25 minutes, until a meat thermometer registers 145°F. to 155°F. (the chops should be a little pink inside). Let stand for 5 minutes before serving with mustard.

Honey-Grilled Pork Tenderloin with Fresh Plum Chutney

Serves 4

3 tablespoons orange juice

2 tablespoons honey

1 tablespoon extra-virgin olive oil

2 teaspoons soy sauce

1 tablespoon Chinese five-spice powder or ground coriander

2 pork tenderloins, 1 pound each

Fresh Plum Chutney (recipe follows), optional

In a large, shallow dish, mix together the juice, honey, oil, soy sauce, and five-spice powder. Pat the tenderloins dry, turn to coat in the marinade, cover with plastic wrap, and refrigerate for 30 minutes or overnight.

Lightly coat a clean grill with cooking oil spray and preheat the grill to medium. Place the tenderloins across the grids, and close the lid. Cook for 5 minutes, then turn the tenderloins on their sides. Cook for another 5 minutes, turning again every 5 minutes until all four sides of the tenderloins are seared (or a total of 20 minutes). Transfer to a cutting board, cover loosely with aluminum foil, and let pork rest for 5 minutes. Slice crosswise into 1/2-inch-thick medallions. Arrange on plates with any accumulated juices and top with the chutney.

Fresh Plum Chutney

Makes about 11/2 cups

1/3 cup peeled and julienned ginger (about 2 ounces gingerroot)

1/4 teaspoon crushed red pepper

Pinch of salt

1/2 cup white vinegar

1/2 cup firmly packed light brown sugar

6 red plums, pitted and thinly sliced

Place the ginger, pepper flakes, salt, vinegar, and brown sugar in a medium skillet over medium heat. Bring to a simmer, stirring to dissolve the sugar. Simmer for 3 minutes, until it begins to look syrupy. Add the plums and stir to coat. Cover and cook for 1 minute, until the plums release their juices. Remove the lid and simmer, uncovered, for 3 minutes, until the plums are just limp (there should be some nice juices and sauce to spoon over the pork).

QUICK SIMPLE IDEA

Pork tenderloins cook quickly on the grill or in a ridged grill pan. For a crowd, double the recipe, slice, and arrange the tenderloins on a platter with a small bowl of the sauce. Tenderloins can be served hot or at room temperature.

Tamarind-Glazed Pork Tenderloins

You can find tamarind pulp, both fresh and frozen, in Asian markets as well as in supermarkets with large Latin-food sections.

Serves 4

2 pork tenderloins, 1 pound each

2 teaspoons ground cumin

1/2 teaspoon salt, plus more to taste

1/2 teaspoon freshly ground black pepper, plus more to taste

1/4 cup orange marmalade

1/4 cup fresh orange juice

1 tablespoon fresh lime juice (from 1 to 2 limes)

1 tablespoon tamarind pulp, seeds removed (or 1 tablespoon molasses mixed with 1/2 teaspoon Worcestershire sauce)

1 tablespoon olive oil

Salt and freshly ground black pepper to taste

Sweet Potato–Chipotle Pancakes (page 62), optional

Pat the tenderloins dry with paper towels. Rub with the cumin, salt, and pepper. Let rest for 15 minutes (or longer in the refrigerator).

Preheat the oven to 425°F.

In a small glass bowl, whisk together the marmalade, orange juice, lime juice, and tamarind and set aside. Heat the oil in a large ovenproof skillet over a medium-high flame. Brown the tenderloins on all sides, 3 to 5 minutes. Remove the pan from the heat and pour the marmalade-tamarind mixture over, turning to coat well. Roast in the oven, basting once or twice, for 20 minutes, or until a meat thermometer inserted in the center reaches 150°F. for medium. Transfer the tenderloins to a platter and cover loosely with foil (the meat should rest for 5 to 10 minutes before carving).

Return the skillet to medium heat and add 3 tablespoons of water. Heat, stirring, until the sauce comes to a simmer. Simmer for about 3 minutes, or until slightly thickened. Stir in any juices that have accumulated on the platter and season with salt and pepper to taste. Slice the meat and arrange on plates with the pancakes, if using. Pour a little of the sauce over each plate.

Spicy Meat and Feta Pizza

Serves 2

10 ounces frozen pizza dough, thawed

Cornmeal, for dusting (optional)

½ pound lean ground sirloin or lamb

3 garlic cloves, minced

½ teaspoon ground cinnamon

¼ teaspoon ground allspice

½ teaspoon salt

¼ teaspoon freshly ground black pepper

1 teaspoon dried oregano, crumbled

½ small red onion, thinly sliced

1 cup cherry tomatoes, halved

½ cup crumbled feta cheese

Preheat the oven to 475°F.

On a well-floured surface, roll out the dough into a 12-inch round and transfer it to an ungreased baking sheet, a 12-inch pizza pan, or a preheated pizza stone lightly dusted with cornmeal. In a medium bowl, combine the raw ground beef with the garlic, cinnamon, allspice, salt, and pepper. Crumble the meat mixture over the dough. Top with the oregano, onion, and tomatoes. Bake for 10 minutes; remove from the oven and scatter the feta over the top. Return to the oven and bake 5 minutes longer, or until the edges of the pie are crisp and lightly brown and the beef is cooked.

QUICK SIMPLE IDEA

Frozen pizza dough is a pretty good substitute for homemade. To defrost pizza dough, thaw it at room temperature for 3 hours, or overnight in the refrigerator. To speed things up, defrost in the microwave: Remove the dough from the package and rub it lightly with oil; place in a resealable plastic bag and pierce a small hole in the bag to allow steam to escape; and microwave on the defrost setting for 3 to 4 minutes, turning the dough over after each minute. Let sit for 2 minutes before rolling out.

Orange Beef and Broccoli Stir-fry

Serves 4

1 tablespoon grated orange zest

1 pound trimmed sirloin steak, cut across the grain into thin 1½-inch-long slices

2 tablespoons canola oil

½ to ¾ teaspoon dried red pepper flakes

3 cloves garlic, minced

1 tablespoon minced fresh ginger

1 small onion, thinly sliced

2 cups small broccoli florets

8 ounces lo mein noodles or linguine (or hot cooked rice)

2 tablespoons fresh orange juice (from about ½ orange)

2 tablespoons low-sodium soy sauce

2 tablespoons hoisin sauce

⅓ cup cashew pieces, toasted

Salt and freshly ground black pepper to taste

In a medium bowl, toss together the zest and steak; set aside. In a large nonstick skillet or wok, heat 1 tablespoon of the oil over a medium-high flame. Add the pepper flakes, garlic, ginger, and onion and stir-fry for 2 to 3 minutes, until the vegetables begin to wilt. Add the broccoli and 2 tablespoons of water; cover and steam for 1 to 2 minutes, until the broccoli is cooked crisp-tender. Transfer to a plate and keep warm.

Cook the noodles according to package directions (about 5 minutes). While the noodles cook, stir together the orange juice, soy sauce, and hoisin sauce. Add the remaining tablespoon of oil to the skillet and return to medium-high heat. Add the beef and cashews and stir-fry for 3 to 4 minutes, until the meat is seared and cooked medium. Return the vegetables to the skillet along with the sauce mixture and stir to combine, about 1 minute. Remove from the heat and season with salt and pepper.

Drain the noodles and divide among 4 bowls. Top with the stir-fry and serve immediately.

QUICK SIMPLE IDEA

To grate the orange rind, use the small holes of a four-sided grater, then tap it on a cutting board to shake off the zest (or use a kitchen rasp).

Coriander Lamb Racks with Blackberry Sauce

This makes a really nice romantic—and easy—dinner for two (which is good, considering how expensive lamb racks are). You need to test the rack starting at about 20 minutes, because if your oven heats unevenly or is smallish, it will cook faster and overcook the lamb—not a good thing. Order the lamb ahead of time and ask the butcher to trim and "french" the bones, removing the meat from the top of the bones, something you probably won't want to do yourself if you want to spend more time being romantic.

Serves 4 to 6

Half 6-ounce package plump blackberries (about ½ cup)

2 teaspoons honey

¼ cup chicken broth

Pinch of ground cardamom

1 tablespoon black peppercorns

1 tablespoon whole coriander seeds

1 teaspoon kosher salt

One 8-bone rack of lamb, about 1½ pounds, trimmed and frenched

2 teaspoons olive oil

Preheat the oven to 425°F.

Combine the berries, honey, broth, and cardamom in a small saucepan over medium-high heat. Bring to a boil, reduce the heat to low, and simmer for 3 minutes, crushing the berries to release their juices. Transfer to a blender and purée. Strain the sauce through a sieve, pushing the sauce through with a spoon. Set aside.

Pulse the peppercorns and coriander seeds in a clean coffee grinder or spice grinder until coarsely ground. Mix the salt into the ground spices. Brush the lamb with the oil and rub all over with the spice mixture. Wrap the bare bones with aluminum foil. Place the lamb fat-side down in a lightly oiled roasting pan in the oven. Roast for 20 to 25 minutes, until a meat thermometer inserted in the center reads 130°F. for medium rare, 140°F. for medium. Transfer to a cutting board and let stand for 5 minutes before carving into double chops. Meanwhile, pour the fat from the pan, add the blackberry sauce, and place it over medium heat. Simmer, stirring, for 1 minute. Stir any accumulated lamb juices into the sauce. Spoon some sauce onto plates, top with the chops, and serve.

Tuscan Peppered Wings

Serves 4 to 6

3 pounds chicken drummettes

2 tablespoons olive oil

2 teaspoons coarsely ground black pepper

1 tablespoon red pepper flakes

1 teaspoon dried thyme

1½ teaspoons kosher salt

2 tablespoons fresh lemon juice (from about
   1 lemon)

Heat the broiler to high and arrange a rack about 6 inches from the heat. Lightly oil a large, heavy baking sheet.

Pat the drummettes dry with paper towels then rub all over with the oil. In a large bowl, mix together the pepper, red pepper flakes, and thyme. Add the wings to the bowl and toss with the spices. Sprinkle with the salt and lemon juice, and let stand for 20 minutes at room temperature (or longer in the refrigerator). Arrange the wings evenly on the prepared baking sheet (don't crowd). Broil until brown and crispy, about 10 minutes (checking every few minutes). Turn the drummettes and broil until brown and crispy and juices run clear, 6 to 8 minutes.

QUICK SIMPLE IDEA

Wings cook fast and get crispy beneath the broiler. They're a great little meal or perfect as party food, especially with Cucumber-Yogurt Salad with Ginger and Mint (page 35).

Real Good Turkey Burgers

I always thought turkey burgers were a bad idea, until I met a caterer who shared her secret to making them delicious—add stuff! This is not only healthier than a beef burger but a lot more delicious. You can fry or grill the burgers and stack on your favorite condiments. The mixture also makes great turkey meatballs—just shape them into golf-ball-size orbs and brown them in a little olive oil.

Serves 4

1 pound ground turkey

1 garlic clove, minced

⅓ cup onion, grated or finely chopped (about ½ medium onion)

2 slices good-quality white bread, cut into cubes

1½ tablespoons white Worcestershire sauce

4 teaspoons olive oil

¾ teaspoon dried oregano, crumbled

½ teaspoon salt

¼ teaspoon freshly ground black pepper

4 whole-wheat hamburger buns, toasted

In a medium bowl, mix together the turkey, garlic, onion, bread, Worcestershire sauce, 2 teaspoons of the olive oil, the oregano, and salt and pepper. Mix well and form into 4 patties.

In a large nonstick skillet, heat the remaining 2 teaspoons of oil over a medium flame until hot but not smoking. Add the burgers and brown on both sides, 1 to 2 minutes on each side (don't press down on burgers with a spatula, which will squeeze out the juice). Add 1 tablespoon of water to the skillet and cover tightly. Cook for 8 to 10 minutes longer, or until the burgers are cooked through and the juices run clear. Transfer to the toasted buns and add condiments as desired.

QUICK SIMPLE IDEA

Grating an onion on the large holes of a four-sided box grater releases its juices and makes it fine enough to cook quickly and nearly melt into the other ingredients. It's a good way to boost the flavor in recipes for meat loaf, meat balls, and salmon patties.

Turkish Meat Loaf

This spicy loaf stuffed with hard-cooked eggs is the ultimate of meat loafs. Serve it hot with Simple Mashed Potatoes (page 59) or cold on a slice of crusty bread with mustard.

Serves 4

3/4 pound ground veal or turkey

3/4 pound ground lamb, pork, or mild sausage

1 cup grated carrots (about 2 medium carrots)

1 small onion, grated

1 garlic clove, minced

1/2 cup chopped parsley

1/2 cup fresh bread crumbs

3 tablespoons milk

1 large egg, beaten

2 teaspoons garam masala or curry powder

1 teaspoon salt

1/4 teaspoon freshly ground black pepper

2 large hard-boiled eggs, shells removed

4 to 5 bacon slices

Preheat the oven to 375°F.

Place all ingredients except the hard-boiled eggs and bacon in a large bowl and use your hands to mix everything thoroughly. Place half the meat mixture into a 9 × 5 × 3-inch glass or metal loaf pan. Center the hard-boiled eggs end to end on top. Enclose the eggs with the remaining meat mixture and form a loaf. Cover the top with the bacon and bake for 35 to 40 minutes, or until the juices run clear. Cool for 10 minutes before slicing.

Herbed Grilled Chicken

Serves 6 to 8

Kosher salt

4 pounds chicken pieces, breasts halved

1 large onion, cut into rings

2 to 3 lemons, thinly sliced

1½ cups loosely packed fresh herb sprigs such as
  flat-leaf parsley, basil, summer savory, lemon
  thyme, oregano, rosemary, or marjoram

3 to 4 tablespoons extra-virgin olive oil

¾ teaspoon freshly ground black pepper

Bring 2 large pots of water to a boil and add salt. Poach the chicken for 15 minutes (less for wings and smaller pieces). Transfer to a colander and let cool for about 10 minutes. In a large, deep platter, layer the warm chicken with the onion, lemon slices, and herbs. Drizzle with some olive oil and sprinkle with 2 teaspoons of salt and the pepper between the layers. Let sit at room temperature for 30 minutes (or cover and refrigerate for longer, or overnight).

Lightly coat a clean grill with cooking oil spray and preheat to medium. Shake off the ingredients from the chicken and place it, skin-side down, on the grill (don't crowd the pieces). Cook for 4 minutes, without turning, to sear. Turn and cook 4 to 5 minutes longer and test for doneness (the chicken should be cooked to an internal temperature of 160°F. to 165°F.).

QUICK SIMPLE IDEA

Cooking raw chicken on the grill usually results in overly charred, dried-out pieces. Poaching the chicken beforehand creates the juiciest possible grilled chicken. This is a great recipe that you can make a day ahead and leave in the fridge until you prepare the fire.

Use a spray bottle with water to extinguish any grill flare-ups. Transfer the cooked chicken to a clean platter (not the one you marinated it on) to prevent contamination. Cook additional lemon halves on the grill with the chicken, cut-side down, and squeeze the juice on the cooked meat.

Chicken with Lemon–Green Olive Sauce

Serves 4 to 6

$^1/_3$ cup all-purpose flour

$^1/_2$ teaspoon salt, plus more to taste

$^1/_4$ teaspoon freshly ground black pepper, plus more to taste

1 to 3 tablespoons olive oil

6 skinless, boneless chicken breast halves, pounded $^3/_4$ inch thick

$^1/_2$ cup thinly sliced shallots

1 cup Simple Chicken Stock (page 94) or low-sodium canned broth

$^1/_2$ cup fresh lemon juice (from about 4 lemons)

1 large lemon, thinly sliced, seeds discarded

$^3/_4$ cup large pitted green olives

1 tablespoon minced fresh thyme or 1$^1/_2$ teaspoons dried

1 tablespoon unsalted butter

On a large plate, stir together the flour, salt, and pepper. Heat 1 tablespoon of the oil in a large nonstick skillet over a medium-high flame. Dredge the chicken in the seasoned flour and sauté in batches, 3 to 4 minutes per side, until cooked through, adding more oil as needed. Transfer to a platter, cover with foil, and keep warm.

Add 1 tablespoon of oil to the same skillet and sauté the shallots for about 1 minute. Add the stock, lemon juice, lemon slices, olives, and thyme and bring to a boil. Reduce the heat to low and simmer until the broth is reduced by half, about 5 minutes. Remove from the heat, and stir in the butter. Drizzle the sauce over the chicken and serve.

Ginger Chicken Satay with Grilled Mango

Serves 4 to 6

2 teaspoons peeled and grated fresh gingerroot

4 garlic cloves, minced

1 teaspoon crushed red pepper

2 teaspoons ground coriander

1½ teaspoons salt

2 tablespoons white wine vinegar

2 teaspoons olive oil

6 skinless, boneless, chicken breast halves (about 2 pounds)

4 ripe mangoes

Satay Sauce (recipe follows)

Special equipment: 20 10- to 12-inch wooden skewers, soaked in water 20 minutes

In a large dish, mix together the ginger, garlic, red pepper, coriander, salt, vinegar, and oil. Slice each chicken breast half lengthwise into 3 to 4 long strips. Add the chicken to the marinade mixture and toss to coat. Cover with plastic wrap and refrigerate for at least 20 minutes, or overnight, if desired.

Lightly coat a clean grill with cooking oil spray and preheat the grill to medium high. Peel the mangoes and slice large pieces from the pits; discard the pits. Remove the chicken from the marinade and thread on skewers. Arrange the skewers diagonally across the grids, without touching. Cook, with the lid down, for 3 minutes per side, until the chicken is seared and just cooked through. Remove to a clean platter and keep warm. Place the mango slices on the grill and cook on both sides until just seared and warm, about 2 minutes per side. Serve with Satay Sauce.

QUICK SIMPLE IDEA

Serve with fragrant jasmine rice, with the rice in the center of a warm platter and the chicken and mango skewers arranged around the rice. Top with a few large cilantro sprigs and lime wedges.

Satay Sauce
Makes about 1¹⁄₄ cups

¹⁄₂ cup unsweetened coconut milk, well stirred

¹⁄₂ cup smooth natural-style peanut butter

1 tablespoon peeled and minced fresh gingerroot

3 tablespoons low-sodium soy sauce

1¹⁄₂ tablespoons light brown sugar

1 tablespoon fresh lemon juice (from about ¹⁄₂ lemon)

¹⁄₂ teaspoon crushed red pepper

Place all the ingredients in a blender or food processor and purée until smooth. The sauce will keep in the refrigerator for up to 5 days.

meat, chicken, fish   **145**

Salt-and-Pepper Roast Cardamom Chicken

To make the chicken more flavorful, prep and marinate it overnight for the following night's dinner.

Serves 4 to 6

4 garlic cloves, chopped

3 tablespoons low-sodium soy sauce

2 tablespoons rice wine vinegar

2 teaspoons honey

$1/4$ teaspoon ground cardamom

3 pounds chicken thighs

$3/4$ teaspoon kosher salt

$3/4$ teaspoon coarsely ground black peppercorns

In a blender, purée the garlic, soy sauce, vinegar, honey, and cardamom. Combine the marinade with the chicken thighs in a resealable plastic bag and marinate at room temperature for 20 minutes (or longer, refrigerated).

Preheat the oven to 425°F. Line a large baking sheet with foil and top with a rack.

Drain the chicken and arrange on the rack without crowding. Sprinkle with the salt and pepper and roast for 20 to 25 minutes, or until the juices run clear.

Teriyaki-Glazed Salmon with Pickled Cucumber Relish

Serves 6

1/3 cup low-sodium teriyaki sauce

1 garlic clove, minced

2 tablespoons minced fresh gingerroot

1 tablespoon brown sugar

1 tablespoon fresh lime juice (from about 1 lime)

6 6-ounce salmon fillets with skins

Pickled Cucumber Relish (recipe follows)

In a large bowl, whisk the teriyaki sauce, garlic, ginger, sugar, and lime juice until the sugar dissolves. Add the salmon, turn to coat, cover with plastic wrap, and refrigerate for 15 to 30 minutes (or overnight).

Lightly coat a clean grill with cooking oil spray and preheat the grill to medium. Arrange the salmon fillets, skin-side down, evenly on the grill, cover, and cook without turning for 8 minutes. Using a large spatula, carefully turn the fillets and cook, covered, 2 to 3 minutes longer, just until the salmon is cooked through but still moist and flaky. Serve with Pickled Cucumber Relish.

Pickled Cucumber Relish
Makes about 1 cup

3/4 cup peeled, seeded, and diced cucumber

2 tablespoons drained pickled ginger, coarsely chopped

1 tablespoon pickled ginger juice

2 tablespoons finely diced red onion, rinsed and drained

1 tablespoon rice wine vinegar

1 tablespoon coarsely chopped fresh cilantro

Salt to taste

Combine the ingredients in a small bowl and toss to combine. Cover and refrigerate until ready to serve.

QUICK SIMPLE IDEA

There are several good brands of teriyaki sauce available, but I prefer Kikkoman. The lighter version has less sugar and sodium with a light, acidic flavor that won't overwhelm the fish. Serve with Wasabi Mashed Potatoes (page 59) and Stir-Fried Greens and Basil (page 55).

Curried Monkfish with Tomatoes and Chilies

Serves 4

1 pound skinless monkfish (or mahi mahi) fillets,
cut into 1½-inch cubes

1 teaspoon finely grated peeled fresh gingerroot

1 teaspoon Indian or ancho chili powder

Salt and freshly ground black pepper

1 tablespoon vegetable oil

⅛ teaspoon mustard seeds

2 green serrano or other small chilies, halved
lengthwise and seeded

2 garlic cloves, minced

4 plum tomatoes, sliced crosswise into ½-inch
pieces

1 tablespoon mango chutney

Ginger and Cardamom–Scented Jasmine Rice
(page 88), optional

Cilantro leaves for garnish

Place the monkfish, ginger, chili powder, and a pinch of salt and pepper in a medium bowl and toss to coat. Let stand at room temperature for 10 minutes (or longer, refrigerated).

Heat the oil in a large nonstick skillet or wok over a medium-high flame. Add the mustard seeds, chilies, and fish and stir-fry for 2 to 4 minutes, until the fish is opaque and cooked through. Transfer the fish to a plate and leave the chilies in the skillet. Add the garlic, tomatoes, and chutney and stir-fry for 2 to 3 minutes, until the tomatoes are heated through but still firm. Return the monkfish to the skillet and stir-fry for 1 to 2 minutes longer, until hot. If desired, remove the chilies before serving with the rice. Top with cilantro leaves.

QUICK SIMPLE IDEA

Monkfish is ideal for a stir-fry because it doesn't break up. This is a sweet-hot Indian-spiced dish that's wonderful with aromatic rice.

Panko-Crusted Fish and Chips

Serves 4

4 skinless fillets of cod, flounder, snapper, or other firm-fleshed white fish (5 to 6 ounces each), about ½-inch thick

2 large eggs beaten with 2 tablespoons water

1½ cups panko (Japanese bread crumbs) or coarse dry bread crumbs

2 to 3 tablespoons peanut oil

Oven Frites (page 62), optional

Kosher salt to taste

Malt vinegar, for serving

Preheat the oven to 425°F. and place a baking sheet with a rack in the center.

Pat the fillets dry with paper towels. Place the egg wash and panko crumbs in shallow bowls. Dip the fillets first in the egg wash, then coat well in the panko crumbs. Let rest on a plate for 10 minutes.

Heat 2 tablespoons of the peanut oil in a large nonstick or cast-iron skillet over a medium-high flame until hot but not smoking. Cook the fillets on both sides until golden brown (add more oil if necessary), 1 to 2 minutes. Transfer the fish to the baking sheet in the oven and roast for 5 to 10 minutes (depending on the thickness of the fish), until just cooked through. Place the fillets on plates with the Oven Frites, if using, sprinkle with salt to taste, and serve with malt vinegar.

Swordfish Masala Kebabs with Mango Raita

Serves 4

2 teaspoons garam masala

1 tablespoon fresh lime juice

1/2 teaspoon salt

3 tablespoons extra-virgin olive oil

1 1/2 pounds swordfish steaks, cut into 1 1/2-inch cubes

1 mango, peeled and coarsely chopped

1 tablespoon chopped fresh mint leaves, plus more for garnish

1 red serrano chili, diced, with seeds

1 tablespoon honey

1/2 cup plain yogurt, preferably whole milk

2 scallions, thinly sliced

Special equipment: 16 10- to 12-inch wooden skewers, soaked in water 20 minutes

In a large bowl, stir together the garam masala, lime juice, salt, and olive oil. Toss the swordfish cubes with the spice marinade and let sit at room temperature for 15 minutes (or longer in the refrigerator). Combine the mango, mint, chili, honey, and yogurt in a blender or food processor and pulse to finely chop. Cover and refrigerate until ready to serve.

Thread 4 to 5 fish cubes on each skewer. Lightly coat a clean grill with cooking spray and preheat to medium high (or prepare a charcoal fire). Arrange the skewers on the diagonal and grill for 2 or 3 minutes per side, until all sides are browned. Sprinkle with the scallions and serve with the mango raita.

Shrimp and Scallop Ceviche

Blood orange juice makes the ceviche more vibrant.

Serves 4 to 6

1 pound bay scallops (or quartered sea scallops)

½ pound peeled and deveined large shrimp, halved lengthwise

3 tablespoons minced red onions

1 jalapeño or serrano chili with seeds, thinly sliced

4 tablespoons fresh lime juice (from 2 to 3 limes)

6 tablespoons fresh orange juice (from 1 to 2 oranges)

2 tablespoons extra-virgin olive oil

2 tablespoons minced fresh cilantro

1 teaspoon salt

1 teaspoon sugar

½ teaspoon chili-garlic paste or habanero chile sauce to taste (optional)

In a medium pot of boiling salted water, add the scallops and shrimp and count to 10. Drain in a colander and briefly rinse beneath cold running water. Combine in a glass bowl with the remaining ingredients. Cover and refrigerate for at least 1 hour, until the seafood is "cooked" by the marinade; do not exceed 8 hours, after which the seafood will toughen.

Sake-Marinated Tuna Steaks with Miso Vinaigrette

Serves 4

1 teaspoon toasted sesame oil

2 tablespoons medium-dry sake

1 tablespoon low-sodium soy sauce

2 teaspoons grated fresh orange zest

1/4 teaspoon freshly ground black pepper

4 6-ounce tuna steaks, 1 inch thick

3 bunches of scallions, ends trimmed (about 20 scallions)

2 teaspoons vegetable oil

Miso Vinaigrette (page 19)

In a small bowl, mix the sesame oil, sake, soy sauce, orange zest, and pepper. Brush both sides of the tuna steaks with the marinade and let sit at room temperature while the grill is heating.

Lightly coat the clean grids with cooking oil spray and preheat to medium high. Brush the scallions lightly with oil, arrange in a single layer on the grill, and cook for 1 to 2 minutes per side with the lid off, until seared and slightly limp. Transfer to a serving platter.

Arrange the tuna steaks evenly across the grill and cook for 3 minutes per side for medium-rare (or 4 minutes per side for medium; 5 minutes or longer for well-done). Turn and cook on the other side to the desired degree of doneness. Place the tuna on top of the scallions, drizzle with the vinaigrette, and serve.

QUICK SIMPLE IDEA

You can make these steaks on an indoor grill or in a hot cast-iron grill pan. You can also substitute another sturdy fish steak, such as swordfish or halibut.

Roasted Whole Snapper on a Bed of Lemons

The cooked lemon slices are delicious eaten with the roasted fish.

Serves 4 to 6

4 large lemons, thinly sliced

Fresh herb sprigs such as oregano, basil, marjoram, rosemary, and thyme (about 2 cups)

1 large (about 4 pounds) or 2 medium whole fish such as red snapper or striped bass, scaled and cleaned, head on or off

2 teaspoons kosher salt

$1/2$ teaspoon freshly ground black pepper

$1/4$ cup extra-virgin olive oil

2 teaspoons crushed fennel seeds

$1/2$ cup dry white wine

Preheat the oven to 425°F.

Line a roasting pan large enough to hold the fish with heavy-duty aluminum foil: The foil needs to be long and wide enough at the edges to form a tent around the fish. Place the sliced lemons in the bottom of the pan and top with half the herbs. Make 2 to 3 diagonal slashes on each side of the fish and sprinkle on both sides with salt and pepper. Place on top of the lemons and herbs. Coarsely chop the remaining herbs in a medium bowl and combine together with the oil and fennel seeds, and drizzle over the fish. Pour in the wine and seal up the sides and ends of the foil. Roast for 35 to 40 minutes, until the fish is just cooked through (allow about 10 minutes per inch of fish thickness). Transfer the fish to a platter and serve with the lemons.

Sole with Tomato-Butter Sauce

Serves 4

8 skinless sole, scrod, or bass fillets (3 to 4 ounces each)

1 teaspoon kosher salt and ¼ teaspoon freshly ground white or black pepper to taste

3 very ripe medium tomatoes, seeded and chopped (substitute cherry tomatoes)

2 tablespoons minced shallot (about 1 shallot)

½ cup dry white wine or vermouth

4 tablespoons cold unsalted butter, cut into 4 pieces, plus more for greasing paper

2 tablespoons fresh lemon juice (from about 1 lemon)

3 tablespoons heavy cream

Preheat the oven to 400°F.

Season the fish with the salt and pepper and arrange in a 9 × 13 × 2-inch glass baking dish. Scatter the tomatoes and shallot over the fish and pour the wine over the top. Butter a piece of wax or parchment paper large enough to cover the dish and place it on top, pressing down lightly. Place the baking dish on a burner, turn the heat to very low, and bring the liquid just to a simmer. Transfer immediately to the oven and bake for 8 to 10 minutes, until the fish is opaque and just cooked through.

Remove the dish from the oven and drain the liquid into a small saucepan (hold an oven mitt against the fish to keep it from sliding). Cover the fish with foil and keep warm while you make the sauce. Bring the liquid to a boil and reduce it until it looks syrupy, about 5 minutes. Add the lemon juice and cream and continue to reduce until the cream thickens, 1 to 2 minutes. Turn down the heat to low and whisk in the butter 1 tablespoon at a time. The sauce should be slightly thick. Taste and season with salt and pepper if necessary. Arrange the fish on warm plates and spoon the sauce over the top.

QUICK SIMPLE IDEA

Baking fish is such an easy task—just don't overdo it—and a gentle way to cook delicate white fillets like sole. This is a simple and lightly rich butter sauce (you only need a drizzle) and not at all complicated.

Barbecued Salmon with Potatoes

Serves 4

1¼ pounds Yukon Gold or red-skinned potatoes, scrubbed and cut into 1-inch cubes

1½ tablespoons olive oil

1 large onion, sliced

1 large red (or yellow) bell pepper, cut into thin strips

1 teaspoon kosher salt, plus more to taste

¼ teaspoon freshly ground black pepper, plus more to taste

1 tablespoon sweet paprika

1 tablespoon brown sugar

¼ teaspoon cayenne

Four 6-ounce skinless salmon fillets or steaks, about 1-inch thick

Partially cook the potatoes by steaming in the microwave or parboiling in boiling salted water for about 8 minutes; set aside.

Preheat the oven to 425°F. In a large, heavy-bottomed, ovenproof skillet, heat the oil over a medium flame. Add the onion and bell pepper and sauté for 5 minutes, until wilted. Remove from the heat and add the potatoes. Season to taste with salt and pepper and toss to incorporate. In a wide, shallow bowl, stir together the paprika, brown sugar, cayenne, salt, and pepper. Roll the fillets in the spice mixture on both sides, shaking off the excess. Place on top of the potato-pepper mixture and slide the skillet in the oven. Roast for 20 to 25 minutes, or until the fillets are firm to the touch and cooked through.

QUICK SIMPLE IDEA

The salmon steaks are also great rubbed with the spices and cooked on a hot grill. If you wish, prepare the potatoes as directed, wrap in aluminum foil, and place on hot coals for a real campfire supper.

Juniper-Steamed Lobster with Ginger Butter

Serves 2

1 tablespoon kosher salt

2 teaspoons crushed juniper berries

2 fresh bay leaves or 1 dried

2 live lobsters (1½ pounds each)

4 tablespoons (½ stick) salted butter

2 heaping teaspoons peeled, finely grated fresh
 gingerroot

Bring a large deep pot of water to a boil
and add the salt, juniper berries, and bay
leaves. Add the lobsters and cover the pot.
Cook for 8 to 10 minutes, until the lobsters
are bright red and the tails are curled under.
Meanwhile, melt the butter in a small
saucepan with the ginger, and transfer to
two small dipping bowls. Halve the lobsters
lengthwise with a large heavy knife, and
serve with the ginger butter.

Quick Simple Paella

Spanish paprika has a distinctive smoke flavor. If you can't locate it, substitute ½ teaspoon smoked ancho chili powder mixed with ½ teaspoon sweet Hungarian paprika.

Serves 4

8-ounce package yellow (Spanish-style) rice

1 cup frozen thawed petit peas

1 3-ounce chorizo sausage link, diced (or other smoked pork sausage)

1 tablespoon olive oil

1 medium onion, chopped

1 red bell pepper, coarsely chopped

2 garlic cloves, minced

1 teaspoon sweet Spanish paprika

¼ teaspoon saffron threads, crushed

½ cup dry white wine

12 large shrimp, shelled and deveined

8 mussels (optional)

1 cup cherry tomato halves

Salt and freshly ground black pepper

3 tablespoons coarsely chopped cilantro

In a medium saucepan, cook the rice according to package directions. Remove from the heat, place the peas on top, and set aside, covered, for 5 minutes.

Meanwhile, in a large nonstick skillet over medium-high heat, brown the sausage and transfer to a plate. Add the oil to the skillet with the onion, bell pepper, garlic, and paprika and sauté over medium heat until the onion is soft, about 3 minutes. Stir the saffron into the wine. Add to the skillet with the shrimp, mussels (if using), and tomatoes, and cook, stirring, until the shrimp are bright pink and the mussels have opened, 2 to 3 minutes. Season to taste with salt and pepper. Add the sausage to the cooked rice and peas and fluff with a fork. Divide the rice among 4 bowls, spoon on the shrimp and juices, and top with cilantro.

QUICK SIMPLE IDEA

To speed things up, buy your shrimp already peeled and deveined or purchase frozen peeled shrimp (uncooked) and thaw in a colander under cold running water.

Thai Curried Mussels in Coconut Broth

Serve the mussels with crusty bread or rice to soak up the rich sauce.

Serves 4

2 tablespoons ($1/4$ stick) unsalted butter

1 large shallot, thinly sliced

2 garlic cloves, minced

1 teaspoon sugar

1 tablespoon Thai red or green curry paste

One and a half 14-ounce cans unsweetened light coconut milk, well stirred

$1/2$ cup dry white wine

4 tablespoons fresh lemon juice (from about $1^{1}/2$ lemons)

2 fresh bay leaves or 1 dried

4 pounds large black mussels, scrubbed and debearded (if necessary)

Salt and freshly ground black pepper to taste

$1/3$ cup coarsely chopped loosely packed flat-leaf parsley

In a large pot over medium heat, melt the butter. Add the shallot and garlic and sauté for about 1 minute, until fragrant. Add the sugar, curry paste, coconut milk, wine, and lemon juice and whisk to dissolve the paste. Add the bay leaves and simmer for 10 minutes. Add the mussels and increase the heat to high. Cover and simmer until the mussels open, 6 to 8 minutes, shaking the pan occasionally. Using a large slotted spoon, transfer the mussels to bowls, discarding any mussels that do not open. Return the sauce to a boil and simmer until slightly thickened, stirring occasionally, about 2 minutes. Season the broth with salt and pepper to taste, discard the bay leaves, and spoon over the mussels. Sprinkle with parsley and serve.

Skewered Shrimp with Duck Sauce

Serves 4

Duck Sauce

¼ cup apricot preserves

1 tablespoon finely minced fresh gingerroot

1 garlic clove, minced

1 tablespoon soy sauce

3 tablespoons white wine vinegar

1 tablespoon habanero or other Caribbean-style pepper sauce

Shrimp

1½ pounds shelled and deveined large shrimp

Lime wedges

Special equipment: Eight to ten 12-inch wooden skewers, soaked in water for 20 minutes

Combine the ingredients for the duck sauce in a small saucepan, add ¼ cup water, and bring to a boil. Lower the heat and simmer, stirring, for 5 minutes. Remove from the heat and transfer to a small bowl to cool.

Lightly spray the grids of a gas or charcoal grill with cooking oil and heat the grill (or a broiler) to high. Thread 3 or 4 shrimp per skewer. Grill for about 2 minutes per side, until the shrimp is pink and just cooked through, transferring them as they cook to a warm platter. Serve the skewers with the duck sauce and a squeeze of lime.

Succotash Sauté with Shrimp

Try this with White Corn Pudding Bread (page 46) for a special summer dinner.

Serves 4 to 6

3 tablespoons unsalted butter

4 cup fresh corn kernels (from 6 to 8 ears)

1 serrano chili, seeded and minced

½ red bell pepper, diced

1 pound medium shrimp, shelled and deveined

3 ounces haricots verts or small string beans, trimmed and steamed tender

6 scallions, finely chopped

½ cup fresh basil or cilantro

Salt and freshly ground black pepper

Melt the butter in a large skillet over medium heat. Sauté the corn, chili, and pepper until tender, about 3 minutes. Add the shrimp, beans, and scallions and cook until the shrimp are bright pink and just cooked through, 3 to 5 minutes. Stir in the basil or cilantro and season with salt and pepper to taste.

desserts

CHOCOLATE

Hot Chocolate Sorbet

Grilled Banana Splits

Chocolate Truffle Sauce

Cowboy Cookies

Chocolate Pudding Cakes

Chocolate Thin Mints

CAKES

Simple Butter Cake

Spicy Double-Ginger Gingerbread

Brown Sugar–Yogurt Cakes

Chocolate Birthday Cake

Chocolate–Sour Cream Frosting

Cookie Crust

Quick Simple Icebox Cheesecake

Upside-Down Pineapple-Cornmeal Cake

PIES AND TARTS

Free-Form Fruit Pies

Basic Piecrust and Four Fillings
PLUM-BERRY PIE FILLING
APRICOT PIE FILLING
APPLE PIE FILLING
BLUEBERRY PIE FILLING

Lemon-Lime Tart

Sweet Pastry Crust

Banana-Chocolate and Pecan Tarts

FRUIT

Baked Candied Apples

Melon and Berry Carpaccio with Honey-Mint Syrup

Summer Fruit in Glasses of May Wine

Vanilla Creamcakes

Strawberries and Cream with Vanilla Creamcakes

Vanilla Custard Cremes with Blackberries

Picture these: easy-bake cakes and open-face rustic pies, hot chocolate sorbet, and the world's best birthday cake topped with pink candles and slick, shiny icing. Chocolate chip–oatmeal cookies and grilled banana splits make you want to skip dinner and indulge in your childhood passions. This collection of unpretentious sweet treats includes little chocolate fixes, creamy frozen creations, and juicy fruits simple enough to make for every day, as well as luscious and playful treats that will impress your guests. None of these is at all difficult to make. Some desserts like cake may take a little longer than others, but this is generally "oven time." So, have dessert—it makes every day a little sweeter.

Hot Chocolate Sorbet

This is homemade chocolate sorbet that's very easy to prepare ahead for a party. Or make a batch to keep in the freezer all for yourself.

Serves 6

$2/3$ cup unsweetened cocoa powder, preferably Dutch process, sifted

1 cup sugar

2 teaspoons instant espresso powder

4 cups whole milk

Whipped cream and shaved chocolate for garnish (optional)

In a large saucepan over medium heat, combine the cocoa, sugar, and espresso powder, then add enough milk to blend into a smooth paste. Add the remaining milk and stir over low heat just until the sugar is dissolved. Pour into ice cube trays and freeze for 8 hours or overnight.

Thaw the cubes for 5 minutes, then empty into a food processor fitted with a metal blade. Process in batches until smooth. Pour into a bowl and refreeze for at least 4 hours. Scoop into bowls or stemmed glasses and serve with whipped cream and chocolate shavings, if using.

Grilled Banana Splits

Serves 4

4 tablespoons (1/2 stick) unsalted butter, melted

1/4 cup packed brown sugar

4 firm-ripe bananas, unpeeled

Vanilla ice cream

Chocolate Truffle Sauce (recipe follows)

1 cup whipped cream

4 maraschino cherries with stems

Preheat the grill to medium high (or prepare charcoals). Combine the butter and sugar in a bowl. Slice the bananas in half lengthwise and brush the butter-sugar mixture on the cut sides of the bananas. Grill the bananas, cut-side down, for 2 to 3 minutes, or until seared and hot. Transfer to a platter, remove the peels, and brush the other side with the butter mixture. Place 2 banana halves each in 4 large, shallow bowls. Arrange 1 to 2 scoops of ice cream in the center, spoon on 2 to 3 tablespoons of Chocolate Truffle Sauce, add a dollop of whipped cream, and top with a cherry.

Chocolate Truffle Sauce

Makes 2 1/2 cups

6 ounces fine-quality bittersweet or semisweet chocolate

4 tablespoons (1/2 stick) unsalted butter

1/2 cup unsweetened cocoa powder

1 1/2 cups heavy cream

5 tablespoons light corn syrup

1/4 cup sugar

Pinch of salt

1 tablespoon dark rum

2 teaspoons vanilla extract

Melt the chocolate and butter in the top of a double boiler over barely simmering water or in a bowl placed in the microwave. Stir in the cocoa powder with a whisk. In a medium saucepan, bring the cream, corn syrup, sugar, and salt to a boil. Remove from the heat and stir in the rum, vanilla, and chocolate mixture. Cool the sauce until almost at room temperature. You can store any leftover sauce in a jar in the refrigerator for up to 1 month.

Cowboy Cookies

Makes about sixteen 3-inch cookies

2 cups all-purpose flour

2 cups whole oats

1/2 teaspoon baking soda

1/2 teaspoon salt

1 cup (2 sticks) unsalted butter, softened

3/4 cup granulated sugar

3/4 cup packed dark brown sugar

2 large eggs

1 teaspoon pure vanilla extract

1 1/2 cups semisweet chocolate chunks or chips

1 cup lightly toasted chopped walnuts or pecans (about 4 ounces)

In a large bowl, stir together the flour, oats, baking soda, and salt. In the large bowl of an electric mixer, beat the butter and sugars until light. Beat in the egg and vanilla. Add the flour-oat mixture and mix just until blended. Fold in the chips and nuts by hand. Place in the freezer for 20 minutes until slightly firm.

Preheat the oven to 350°F. Lightly spray a large cookie sheet with vegetable oil or line it with parchment paper or aluminum foil. Scoop about 1/4 cup of cookie dough and roll it in your hand to form a ball (or use a small ice cream scoop). Place it on the prepared cookie sheet and slightly flatten with your hand, leaving about 1 inch between the cookies. Bake the cookies for about 8 minutes. Remove the cookie sheet, rotate it, return to the oven, and bake for 8 to 10 minutes more, or until the cookies are golden brown around the edges and no longer soft in the center. Cool on sheets for 5 minutes before transferring to racks to cool completely. The cookies will stay fresh in an airtight container for up to a week.

QUICK SIMPLE IDEA

This recipe comes from my friend Toni Allocca's take-out gourmet shop, Olive's, in SoHo. Making these is a good weekend project that doesn't take much time and saves you some embarrassment for those parental get-togethers where it's considered bad form to bring a box of Entenmann's. Make the dough and use a small ice cream scoop to make round balls. Place them on a wax- or parchment-lined baking sheet and freeze them until solid.

Then place the balls in plastic freezer bags. Whenever you want to make cookies, simply place them on lined baking sheets and bake as directed (it takes a little longer if they're frozen solid).

Chocolate Pudding Cakes

Serves 6

4 tablespoons (1/2 stick) unsalted butter

1 cup granulated sugar

2 large eggs

1 teaspoon pure vanilla extract

1 cup all-purpose flour

1 cup unsweetened cocoa powder

1 teaspoon baking powder

1/2 teaspoon salt

1/2 cup packed dark brown sugar

Confectioners' sugar for dusting

Vanilla or coffee ice cream

Preheat the oven to 350°F. Butter six 8-ounce ironstone coffee cups (not fine china), ramekins, or custard cups. (If using cups, you will also need saucers.)

In a 2-quart saucepan, heat the butter until melted; cool slightly. Beat in the granulated sugar, eggs, and vanilla. In a medium bowl, stir together the flour, 3/4 cup of the cocoa powder, baking powder, and salt. Beat the flour mixture into the butter-sugar mixture with a wire whisk until there are no visible lumps. Divide the batter evenly among the cups and place the cups in their saucers on a large baking sheet.

Bring 3/4 cup of water to a boil. In a small bowl, whisk together the brown sugar, the remaining 1/4 cup of cocoa powder, and the boiling water. Pour over the cake batter, dividing evenly among the cups. Bake for 25 to 30 minutes, until the cakes are puffed and firm at the edges (they should still be soft at the center). Cool for 15 minutes and dust lightly with confectioners' sugar. Serve warm with ice cream.

QUICK SIMPLE IDEA
Baking these in individual coffee cups makes an adorable presentation for a dinner party. Though it's less attractive, you can also bake it in an 8-inch square pan and spoon it into bowls. This is very rich, so ice cream is a must to cut the deep chocolate flavor.

Chocolate Thin Mints

To make this, you will need peppermint oil specially formulated for candy making (available from candy and cake-decorating supply stores).

Makes 32 pieces

12 ounces semisweet chocolate chips

6 ounces white chocolate chips

2 to 3 drops peppermint oil (do not use extract or essential oil)

3 to 4 drops green food coloring (optional)

Line an 8-inch square baking pan with aluminum foil, leaving a 1-inch overlay. In a bowl set over barely simmering water or in a microwave, heat the semisweet chocolate until half the chips are melted. Remove from the stove and stir until completely melted and smooth. Spread half the semisweet chocolate evenly in the bottom of the pan. Refrigerate for 5 to 10 minutes.

Meanwhile, heat the white chocolate in the same manner until half melted. Remove from the heat and stir until completely melted. Stir in the peppermint oil and food coloring (if using) until blended. Spread over the cooled chocolate. Refrigerate for 10 minutes until firm.

Reheat the remaining semisweet chocolate if necessary, and spread over the cooled white chocolate layer. Refrigerate until solid. Grasping the foil, lift the chocolate from the pan and transfer to a cutting board; peel away the foil. With a heavy, sharp knife, cut into sixteen 2-inch squares, then cut the squares into triangles or simply break into pieces. (The chocolate will keep, refrigerated, for up to 5 days or, frozen, for up to 1 month.)

Simple Butter Cake

Makes one 9-inch round or 8-inch square cake or 1 dozen cupcakes

9 tablespoons unsalted butter, softened, plus more for greasing pan

1 cup all-purpose flour, plus more for dusting pan

1 teaspoon baking powder

1/4 teaspoon salt

3/4 cup granulated sugar

2 large eggs, room temperature

1 teaspoon pure vanilla extract

1/3 cup plus 1 tablespoon whole milk, at room temperature

Confectioners' sugar for dusting

QUICK SIMPLE IDEA

This is a versatile plain cake. You can slice it in half and layer it to make 4 wedges; dust it with confectioners' sugar and serve the wedges with sweetened strawberries and whipped cream; or make cupcakes and spread them with Chocolate–Sour Cream Frosting (page 178).

Preheat the oven to 350°F. Butter a 9-inch round or 8-inch square baking pan. Line the bottom with parchment paper or wax paper and butter the paper. Lightly dust the inside of the pan with flour.

In a medium bowl, sift together the flour, baking powder, and salt. In the large bowl of an electric mixer, cream 6 tablespoons of the butter and granulated sugar on medium-high speed for 3 minutes, until fluffy. Add the eggs and vanilla and beat well. On the lowest speed, alternately add the flour mixture and the milk, scraping down the sides, just until the ingredients are combined.

Spoon the batter into the pan. Bake for 25 to 30 minutes (16 to 18 minutes for cupcakes), or until a wooden toothpick inserted into the center of the cake comes out clean and the cake is pulled slightly away from the pan. Cool on a rack for 5 minutes. Carefully invert the cake onto a rack and peel away the paper. Invert again to let it cool right side up. When cool, transfer to a serving plate. Spread the top and sides with a thin layer of the remaining 3 tablespoons of softened butter and dust the cake all over with confectioners' sugar. Cut the cake in half horizontally, top one half with a thin layer of softened butter, and top with the other half to make 2 layers. Cut into 4 wedges, dust with more sugar, and serve.

Spicy Double-Ginger Gingerbread

Makes nine 2¹/₂-inch squares

1 2-inch-long piece peeled fresh gingerroot, coarsely chopped

1¹/₂ teaspoons baking soda

¹/₂ cup (1 stick) unsalted butter, softened

¹/₂ cup blackstrap molasses

³/₄ cup packed dark brown sugar

1 large egg

1¹/₂ cups all-purpose flour

2 teaspoons baking powder

¹/₂ teaspoon salt

2 teaspoons ground ginger

1 teaspoon ground cinnamon

1 teaspoon freshly grated nutmeg

Confectioners' sugar for dusting

Preheat the oven to 350°F. Grease and flour an 8-inch square baking pan.

Bring ¹/₂ of cup water and the fresh ginger to a boil in a small pan. Remove from the heat, cover, and steep for 10 minutes. Strain, add the baking soda, and set aside.

Beat the butter, molasses, and brown sugar with an electric mixer until very creamy. Beat in the egg. In a medium bowl, stir together the flour, baking powder, salt, ground ginger, cinnamon, and nutmeg. With the mixer on low, gradually add the ginger water to the butter mixture, then add the dry ingredients, mixing until just blended. Scrape the batter into the prepared pan and bake for 50 to 55 minutes, or until a wooden skewer inserted in the center comes out clean. Place on a rack to cool completely. Cut into squares and lightly dust with confectioners' sugar before serving.

QUICK SIMPLE IDEA

The secret to great gingerbread is using fresh spices. The spice should be quite pungent when you open the jar. If not, either use about twice as much or purchase a new jar (spices usually last 6 months to a year).

Brown Sugar–
Yogurt Cakes

Makes 6 cakes

1/4 cup packed brown sugar

1/3 cup sliced toasted almonds

1 teaspoon ground cinnamon

6 tablespoons (3/4 stick) unsalted butter, melted, plus more for greasing pan

1/2 cup granulated sugar

2 large eggs, beaten

1 teaspoon pure vanilla extract

11/4 cups all-purpose flour

1 teaspoon baking powder

1/2 teaspoon baking soda

3/4 cup plain yogurt

3 tablespoons confectioners' sugar

Preheat the oven to 325°F. Butter all surfaces of a 6-cup mini Bundt pan (with 1-cup molds).

Make the filling: In a medium bowl, mix together the brown sugar, almonds, and cinnamon. Set aside.

Make the cake: In a small bowl, beat together the melted butter, granulated sugar, eggs, and vanilla. Place the flour, baking powder, and baking soda in a large bowl. Add the egg mixture and the yogurt and stir just until blended. Place about 2 tablespoons of the batter in the bottoms of the Bundt cups. Divide the brown sugar filling evenly among the cups. Fill the cups with the remaining batter, about three-quarters full. Bake for 25 to 30 minutes, until the cakes are firm to the touch and the edges are brown and pulled away from sides of pan. Allow to cool for 5 minutes in the pan before turning out on a rack. Cool, flat-side down, to room temperature. Before serving, lightly dust with the confectioners' sugar.

QUICK SIMPLE IDEA

If you don't have a mini Bundt pan, you can bake these in a large muffin tin. Sprinkle the brown sugar–almond mixture on top for a crumb crust.

Chocolate Birthday Cake

**Makes one 2-layer 8-inch cake or one
9 × 13 × 2-inch cake**

²/₃ cup unsweetened cocoa powder

¹/₂ cup (1 stick) unsalted butter, at room
    temperature, plus more for greasing pans

1¹/₂ cups granulated sugar

2 large eggs

1¹/₄ teaspoons pure vanilla extract

1¹/₂ cups cake flour, plus more for dusting pan

¹/₂ teaspoon baking powder

1 teaspoon baking soda

¹/₂ teaspoon salt

Chocolate–Sour Cream Frosting (page 178)

Preheat the oven to 350°F. Line the bottoms of two 8-inch round cake pans with wax paper and butter and flour the bottoms and sides well.

Bring 1 cup water to a boil. In a medium bowl, whisk together the cocoa powder and boiling water until smooth; set aside. Place the butter, sugar, eggs, and vanilla in a large bowl. Using an electric mixer, beat for 2 minutes, until very light and fluffy. In another bowl, sift together the flour, baking powder, baking soda, and salt. Add to the butter mixture in three parts alternately with the cocoa mixture.

Pour and scrape the batter into the prepared pans and bake for 22 to 25 minutes, or until the cakes have slightly pulled away from the sides of the pan and a toothpick inserted in the center comes out clean (or with just a few crumbs clinging to it); the cake should be fudgy and moist but not dry, so don't overbake. Cool in the pans for 10 minutes, then turn out onto cake racks to cool completely. Frost with Chocolate–Sour Cream Frosting.

QUICK SIMPLE IDEA

Make the cake early in the day so that it will be completely cooled when you're ready to frost it. Pink birthday candles look especially pretty with the dark frosting.

Chocolate–Sour Cream Frosting

This is a rich, glossy frosting that stays soft and creamy and never gets firm. Make it just before you're ready to frost your cake.

Makes enough to frost a two-layer 8-inch cake

1 12-ounce package semisweet chocolate chips

1 cup sour cream (don't use reduced-calorie or nonfat), at room temperature

Pinch of salt

Melt the chocolate in a small bowl in the microwave or over a pan of barely simmering water until half melted. Remove from the heat and continue stirring until smooth. Add the sour cream and salt and stir until thoroughly blended; the frosting should be thick enough to spread easily. Spread the frosting on the cake while the frosting is still a bit warm.

Cookie Crust

Makes one 9-inch crust

1/4 cup (1/2 stick) unsalted butter, melted, plus more for greasing dish

1/2 teaspoon pure almond extract

2 cups vanilla wafer cookie crumbs

Preheat the oven to 325°F. and butter a 9-inch glass pie dish.

In a medium bowl, combine the melted butter, almond extract, and cookie crumbs and use your hands to firmly press the crumb mixture onto the bottom and up the sides of the pie dish. Bake until lightly toasted, about 10 minutes. Set aside to cool completely.

Quick Simple Icebox Cheesecake

A light and easy way to a fast cheesecake fix.

Serves 6 to 8

1 8-ounce package cream cheese, at room temperature

$1/3$ cup confectioners' sugar

$1/2$ cup heavy cream

1 teaspoon pure vanilla extract

$1/2$ teaspoon pure almond extract

Cookie Crust (at left)

1 or 2 ripe peaches, thinly sliced

2 ripe kiwis, peeled and sliced $1/4$ inch thick

1 $1/2$ pint-basket fresh blackberries or raspberries

$1/4$ cup red currant jam (optional)

Make the filling: Blend the cream cheese with an electric mixture until smooth. Add the sugar, cream, vanilla, and almond extract and blend until creamy and slightly whipped up (don't beat too much or the filling will become too mousselike). Spread the filling in the cooled crust and refrigerate until firm, about 3 hours. (The pie can be prepared to this point 1 day ahead, covered with plastic wrap, and refrigerated until ready to serve.)

An hour or two before you're ready to serve the pie, arrange the peach slices, then the kiwi slices, in concentric circles from the edge of the crust toward the center, leaving a circle in the center to place the berries. Heat the jam, if using, until it's melted and lightly brush the fruit with a thin coating to glaze it. Refrigerate for up to 3 hours, or until ready to serve.

QUICK SIMPLE IDEA

You can also use a purchased cookie crust to make the cheesecake. Use any favorite fruit to decorate the top—just make sure it's at its peak. Nectarines, plums, bananas, strawberries, or star fruit are pretty arranged in a concentric circle around the top.

Upside-Down Pineapple-Cornmeal Cake

Serves 6

10 tablespoons (1¼ sticks) unsalted butter

½ cup packed dark brown sugar

1 20-ounce can pineapple slices, drained

6 pecan halves (optional)

½ cup whole milk

1 large egg

¼ cup white or yellow cornmeal

1 cup all-purpose flour

½ cup granulated sugar

1 teaspoon baking powder

½ teaspoon salt

Preheat the oven to 350°F.

Melt 3 tablespoons of the butter in a 10-inch cast-iron skillet (or other heavy, ovenproof pan). Sprinkle the brown sugar in the skillet and arrange 6 or 7 pineapple slices on top. Cut the other slices in half moons and arrange around the sides of the pan. Place the nuts, if using, in the center of the pineapple rings.

Place the remaining 7 tablespoons of butter in a medium saucepan over low heat and stir until half melted; remove from the heat. Add the milk and egg and whisk together. Stir in the cornmeal, flour, granulated sugar, baking powder, and salt until just blended. Scrape the batter into the skillet over the pineapple slices and spread evenly to cover. Bake for 25 to 30 minutes, until the cake is golden and firm to the touch. Cool in the skillet for 10 minutes.

To unmold, place a large platter over the skillet and quickly flip over (if pineapple slices stick to the skillet, lift them off with a spatula and place them on the cake). Serve immediately.

Free-Form Fruit Pies

Making your own pie is infinitely better than using what you can find in the freezer case or the bakery. But there's no need to fuss over a lattice crust or perfectly crimped edges: You can make a perfectly good pie by rolling out the dough, pizza fashion, and folding the edges about the fruit. Here is a very simple recipe for a piecrust made in a food processor. Or, you can use a prepared crust for the job—the type you find in the market's refrigerator case. Serve hot with ice cream, if desired.

Serves 6 to 8

Basic Piecrust (page 182) or 1 refrigerated piecrust

1 batch fruit filling (pages 182–183)

1/2 tablespoon unsalted butter, cut into small pieces

Confectioners' sugar for dusting

Preheat the oven to 400°F.

Let the dough sit at room temperature for 10 minutes. Roll out on a lightly floured surface with a floured rolling pin into a 13-inch circle. Fold into quarters, then fold out onto a baking sheet or a 10-inch pie plate. Chill while you make the filling.

Arrange the filling evenly in the center of dough, leaving a 2-inch border. Fold the edges of the dough around the fruit to form the sides of the pie. Dot with butter, and bake for 30 to 40 minutes, until the crust is lightly golden and the fruit is bubbling. Cool for 10 minutes and dust lightly with sugar before serving.

Basic Piecrust and Four Fillings

Makes one 9-inch crust

1¼ cups all-purpose flour

¼ teaspoon salt

6 tablespoons (¾ stick) cold, unsalted butter, cut into small pieces

2 tablespoons cold vegetable shortening

3 to 4 tablespoons ice water

Place the flour, salt, butter, and shortening in a food processor and pulse for 30 seconds, until the mixture resembles coarse crumbs. Sprinkle ice water over the dough and pulse for about 10 seconds, until the dough just begins to stick together (it will still be crumbly). Scrape out onto a large piece of plastic wrap, gather into a rough ball, and wrap in the plastic. Press into a flat, 1-inch disk (like a large burger) and refrigerate for at least 30 minutes before rolling.

Plum-Berry Pie Filling

1½ pounds ripe plums or nectarines (or peeled peaches), pitted and sliced ¼ thick

1 cup raspberries or blackberries

½ cup sugar

1 tablespoon fresh lemon juice (from about ½ lemon)

1 tablespoon all-purpose flour

Toss all ingredients in a bowl.

Apricot Pie Filling

4 8-ounce cans apricot halves in heavy syrup, drained

2 tablespoons sugar

1 teaspoon pure vanilla extract

1 tablespoon all-purpose flour

Toss all the ingredients in a bowl. To form the pie, arrange the apricot halves cut-side down.

Apple Pie Filling

1^1/$_2$ pounds apples, such as Granny Smith or
    Golden Delicious, peeled, cored, and sliced
    ^{1}/$_4$ inch thick

^{1}/$_2$ cup packed dark brown sugar

1 teaspoon ground cinnamon

2 tablespoons fresh lemon juice (from about
    ^{1}/$_2$ lemon)

1 tablespoon all-purpose flour

Toss all the ingredients in a bowl.

Blueberry Pie Filling

3 cups fresh blueberries

^{1}/$_4$ cup sugar

1 tablespoon fresh lemon juice (from about
    ^{1}/$_2$ lemon)

2 teaspoons finely grated fresh lemon zest

1 tablespoon all-purpose flour

Toss all the ingredients in a bowl.

Lemon-Lime Tart

This recipe was given to me by my friend Lori Longbothom (author of *Luscious Lemon Desserts*, Chronicle, 2001).

Makes one 11-inch tart

1 recipe Sweet Pastry Crust (recipe follows)

1 cup sugar

6 large eggs

½ cup heavy cream

½ cup fresh lime juice (from 6 to 8 limes)

¼ cup fresh lemon juice (from about 3 lemons)

2 teaspoons freshly grated lime zest

Confectioners' sugar for dusting

Make the tart shell and bake as directed. Cool and set aside (this can be done earlier in the day, if desired). Preheat the oven to 350°F. and arrange a rack in middle of the oven.

In a large bowl, whisk together the sugar and eggs until well blended. Slowly whisk in the cream, juices, and zest until smooth and creamy. Partially pull out the oven rack and place the tart shell on the rack. Carefully pour in the cream filling (it will be very runny). Bake for 25 to 30 minutes, until the tart is set around the edges but still a little wobbly in the center. Cool for at least 1 hour (the center will have firmed up). Dust lightly with confectioners' sugar before serving.

QUICK SIMPLE IDEA

You can make the tart pastry and freeze it in the pan even weeks before you plan to serve it. Arrange a few raspberries, blackberries, or fresh currants (if you can find them) around the edges and on top of the tart.

Sweet Pastry Crust

Makes one 11-inch tart shell

1/2 cup (1 stick) cold unsalted butter, cut into
    small pieces

1/2 cup confectioners' sugar

Pinch of salt

1 1/2 cups all-purpose flour

1 large egg yolk

1 to 2 tablespoons cold milk or water

Preheat the oven to 350°F.

Place the butter, sugar, salt, flour, and egg
yolk in the bowl of a food processor and
pulse a few times until the mixture
resembles coarse meal. Add the milk and
pulse two or three times, until the dough
comes together. Scrape into an 11-inch tart
pan. Flour your fingertips and lightly press
the dough on the bottom and sides of the
pan until it is evenly distributed. Place in
the freezer for 15 minutes, until firm. Bake
the tart for 20 minutes, until lightly golden,
and cool on a rack.

Banana-Chocolate and Pecan Tarts

These are wonderfully simple tarts made with frozen puff pastry from the supermarket that taste as if you bought them in a fancy bakery. Splurge on a good bar of French or Swiss chocolate —it makes all the difference.

Serves 4

1 sheet frozen puff pastry, thawed but still cold

Flour for dusting

3 ounces fine-quality bittersweet or semisweet chocolate, finely chopped

2 large, firm-ripe bananas, diagonally sliced 1/4 inch thick

1/2 cup lightly toasted chopped pecans or walnuts

4 tablespoons sugar

2 tablespoons cold unsalted butter, cut into small pieces

Vanilla ice cream (optional)

Preheat the oven to 425°F.

Unfold the pastry sheet on a lightly floured surface and slice it in half. Roll each half out into a 10 x 5-inch rectangle. Cut each rectangle in half to form four 5-inch squares. Arrange the squares on two large baking sheets about 2 inches apart. Sprinkle the squares evenly with the chocolate, leaving a 1/2-inch border along the edges. Beginning from the outside edges and working to the center, arrange the banana slices—slightly overlapping—into a square pattern so that the top of the tart is covered. Sprinkle evenly with the nuts, sugar, and butter pieces. Chill in the refrigerator for 15 minutes.

Bake the tarts in the middle of the oven, in batches if necessary, for 10 to 15 minutes, or until the pastry is golden brown on the bottom and cooked through. Serve the tarts at room temperature or warm with vanilla ice cream, if using.

Baked Candied Apples

This is so simple, and a comforting home-cooked dessert served hot with melting vanilla or caramel ice cream.

Serves 4

4 large Gala or Golden Delicious apples

3 tablespoons brown sugar

1^1/$_2$ teaspoons ground cinnamon

4 cinnamon sticks

^{1}/$_4$ cup apple or red currant jelly

1 cup apple cider

Vanilla or dulce de leche ice cream (optional)

Preheat the oven to 375°F.

Core the apples from the stem ends, leaving a little of the bottoms intact to form a well. Peel the apples halfway to their middles and arrange in a shallow baking dish. In a small bowl, mix together the sugar and cinnamon and sprinkle over the apples. Place a cinnamon stick in each. Bring the jelly and cider to a boil in a small saucepan, stirring to dissolve the jelly. Drizzle over the apples and bake, basting occasionally, for 30 minutes, or until tender. Serve hot with ice cream, if using.

Melon and Berry Carpaccio with Honey-Mint Syrup

These colors are gorgeous. You could use a mandoline to obtain extra-thin melon slices.

Serves 4

1 lemon

1 lime

$1/3$ cup mild-flavored honey

$1/2$ cup coarsely chopped mint, plus more for garnish

$1/2$ ripe cantaloupe

$1/2$ ripe honeydew

$1/2$ cup plump blackberries or sliced strawberries

With a vegetable peeler, remove the bright yellow and green parts only from the rinds of the lemon and lime. Juice and strain the lemon and lime. Place the rinds, juice, and honey in a small saucepan and bring to a boil, stirring to dissolve the honey. Remove from the heat and stir in the chopped mint. Set aside to cool to room temperature.

Cut medium wedges from the melons and cut away the rind and tough green flesh. Using a sharp knife or mandoline, follow the curve and make long, thin slices. Arrange on a platter and place in the refrigerator until ready to use. Arrange the berries on top of the melon, drizzle lightly with the honey syrup, and garnish with mint.

Summer Fruit in Glasses of May Wine

Super-ripe summer fruit is the simplest of all desserts. Slice peaches, nectarines, plums, and figs and place them in a wineglass. Fill with a dessert wine such as May wine, late-harvest Riesling, or Sauternes. Serve in your favorite glasses with ginger cookies.

Vanilla Creamcakes

Makes 12 shortcakes

1/2 cup heavy cream, plus more for brushing

3/4 cup whole milk

1 large egg

1 teaspoon pure vanilla extract

1 vanilla bean, seeds scraped (optional)

3 cups plus 1 tablespoon all-purpose flour, plus more for dusting

1/4 cup confectioners' sugar

1 tablespoon plus 2 teaspoons baking powder

3/4 teaspoon cream of tartar

3/4 teaspoon salt

3/4 cup (1 1/2 sticks) cold unsalted butter, cut into small pieces

Preheat the oven to 400°F.

Whisk together the cream, milk, egg, and vanilla extract and vanilla bean and seeds (if using). In a large bowl, stir together the flour, sugar, baking powder, cream of tartar, and salt. Work the butter into the flour mixture with your fingertips until it resembles coarse meal. Stir in the cream mixture until it forms a dough.

Turn out onto a lightly floured surface and gently knead for 30 seconds. Roll or lightly pat the dough to a 1-inch thickness. Using a large biscuit cutter, cut into 3-inch rounds. Place on an ungreased baking sheet (or one lined with parchment paper or foil) about 1 inch apart; bake in batches, if necessary, for 10 to 12 minutes, or until lightly brown on top. Serve warm or at room temperature.

QUICK SIMPLE IDEA
Prepare these vanilla-flavored shortcakes ahead of time and let them bake while you clear the dinner table. Serve warm with sliced peaches, fresh sweetened berries, or homemade preserves and butter.

Strawberries and Cream with Vanilla Creamcakes

Serve the berries and cream solo or make warm Vanilla Creamcakes to go with them.

Serves 6

2 pints small ripe strawberries, hulled and sliced

2 to 3 tablespoons sugar, depending on the sweetness of the berries

2 tablespoons fresh lemon juice (from about 1 lemon)

1 cup well-chilled heavy cream

2 tablespoons confectioners' sugar

$1/4$ cup sour cream

Vanilla Creamcakes (page 190), optional

In a medium bowl, combine the berries with the sugar and lemon juice. Toss to combine and allow to macerate in the refrigerator for 1 hour. In a chilled bowl, beat the heavy cream with the confectioners' sugar until it holds soft peaks. Beat in the sour cream until the mixture is stiff. Serve with the berries and creamcakes, if using.

Vanilla Custard Cremes with Blackberries

Serves 4

1 pint (2 cups) half-and-half

1/3 cup plus 2 tablespoons sugar

Pinch of salt

1 envelope plain gelatin

1/2 teaspoon pure vanilla extract

2 6-ounce containers fresh blackberries

1 tablespoon fresh lemon juice (from about 1/2 lemon)

In a large saucepan over medium-high heat, bring the half-and-half, 1/3 cup of sugar, and salt to a boil. Remove immediately from the heat. Sprinkle the gelatin over the mixture and whisk until dissolved. Stir in the vanilla. Pour the mixture though a fine-mesh strainer into a large measuring cup. Divide the mixture evenly among four 6-ounce glass custard cups. Cool to room temperature, cover each cup with plastic wrap, and refrigerate for at least 2 hours, until firm, or overnight. (The custards can be made up to 2 days ahead and kept refrigerated.)

In a medium bowl, toss the blackberries with the remaining 2 tablespoons of sugar and the lemon juice. Let stand for 15 minutes (or up to 2 hours), then mash some of the berries to release their juices. Gently loosen the edges of the custards with the end of a butter knife. Dip the bottoms of the cups briefly in hot water and invert onto the dessert plates. Spoon the blackberries and syrup around the custards.

QUICK SIMPLE IDEA

This no-egg custard resembles *panna cotta* with a delicate texture and vanilla flavor.

Acknowledgments

The great thing about writing a cookbook is they let you have a whole page to thank the people who helped you do it, some of them unknowingly. The following folks deserve more than that for their inspiration, friendship, and good stomachs. If you are very lucky, you have a mom and dad and sister like mine (Emma, Jim, and Linda), always there to listen when I needed a shoulder to cry on (or a good kick). Special thanks with whipped cream on top to Angela Miller, who has been much more than an agent but also a good friend whose gentle nudging I have appreciated these last few years. I'd like to thank everyone at Clarkson N. Potter, a group of very creative people who know what it takes to make a cookbook happen (which is neither quick nor simple). This includes my skillful and patient editor, Chris Pavone, Pam Krauss, Marysarah Quinn, Caitlin Daniels Israel, Lauren Shakely, and Sibylle Kazeroid.

I am especially grateful to Susan Wyland, the founding editor of *Real Simple* magazine, for her friendship and encouragement along the way, as well as for giving me the opportunity in those pages to show how simple food could be both beautiful and delicious. At *Health* magazine, Doug Crichton and Lisa Delaney have also given me free rein in the recipe (and life) departments (which is wonderful in itself), and have always been more than understanding of my dual career.

Merci beaucoup to Lisa Rutledge—a great friend for years and now a photographic genius—for the beautiful photos that make the book so much better than it would have been without her careful eye. My heartfelt thanks to official tasters and good friends Kathy Snyder and Mike Hylton of Ventura Farm in Shelbyville, Kentucky.

Thanks too to my Kentucky equine friends in the American Saddlebred world, for the many lessons of horsemanship and many more laughs and good times. *Grazie mille* to my handsome friends Caleb Negron and Robert Triefus, for the use of their stylish farmhouse in Buck's County as a backdrop for the photos in the book.

My years as a magazine editor at food and women's publications were spent with the smartest, wisest, and most creative people I know (many of whom were generous with the assignments that helped fund my book-writing career). They include Susan Barr at *Self*, Sally Belk King at *Bon Appétit*, Judy Coyne of *Good Housekeeping*, the late Michelle Fleischer, Amy Gross at *O*, Mary Ann Howkins, Carol Kramer at *Rosie*, Kristine Kidd at *Bon Appétit*, Cindi Leive at *Glamour*, Jill Melton at *Cooking Light*, Peggy Northrup at *Organic Style*, Suzy Lilly Ott, Susan Spungen at *Martha Stewart Living*, and Susan Westmoreland at *Good Housekeeping*.

Other friends and mentors, past and present, whose advice and support I greatly appreciate are Toni Allocca, Mark Bittman, Rebecca Benton, Giuliano Bugialli, Daniel Combs, Kerri Conan, Karin Eaton, Shawn Ehlers, Mark Ferri, David Greenbaum, James Hunter, Lori Longbotham, Marilyn MacFarlane, chef extraordinaire Ouita Michel, the late Minnie Pearl, Barbara Moutenot, Susie Wolfe Query, John Sessler, Lorelei Shellist, Beth Stein, Bonnie Stern, Aaron Wax, and Rand Wohlstetter.

Index

Note: Pages in *italics* refer to photographs.

A

Apple(s)
Baked Candied, 187
–Butternut Squash Soup, 102
and Goat Feta, Baby Spinach with, 34
Pie Filling, 183
Apricot Pie Filling, 182
Arugula, Linguine with Walnuts and, 70
Asian Spiced Fruit, 27
Asparagus, Penne, and Ham Frittata, 76, 77
Asparagus with Prosciutto-Bacon and Eggs, 48, 48
Avocado(s)
Poached Chicken, and Citrus Salad, 23
Simple Guacamole, 126
and Smoked Salmon Salad, 35
Spring Chopped Salad with Lime-Mint
Vinaigrette, 32, 33

B

baking sheets, 9
Balsamic-Shallot Vinaigrette, 42
Banana(s)
-Chocolate and Pecan Tarts, 186
Asian Spiced Fruit, 27
Splits, Grilled, 167
Barbecued Salmon with Potatoes, 159
Barley and Roasted Corn Pilaf, 83
Basil
Mashed Potatoes, 59
Simple Pesto, 50
Stir-Fried Greens and, 55
Vinegar, Sweet, Heirloom Tomato Salad with, 31
Basmati Rice, Coconut, 78
Bean(s)
Black, Salad, Warm, Cumin Chicken with, 43
Black, Spicy, 83
Cabbage, Carrot, and Chickpea Salad, 28, 29
Green Thai Vegetable Curry, 51
Lentil-Rice Soup, 107
Lima, and Chickpeas with Warm Bacon Dressing, 36, 37
Quinoa-Edamame Pilaf, 86
Salt-Baked Crushed Potatoes with Lentils and Fried
Onions, 60, 61
Spring Chopped Salad with Lime-Mint Vinaigrette, 32, 33
Stewed Lentils with Chorizo and Queso Fresco, 116, 117
Succotash Sauté with Shrimp, 163
Vegetable and Shrimp Curry, 51
Vegetarian Chili with Grilled Polenta, 110
White, –Escarole Soup with Polenta Croutons, 108, 109
Beef
Cowboy Steaks with Pico de Gallo, 122
Grilled London Broil with Green Olive Tapenade, 123
Orange, and Broccoli Stir-Fry, 135
Perfect Grilled Steak, 124, 125
Plantains with Picadillo, 127
Rosemary-Wrapped Filet Mignon, 128, 129
Spicy Cinnamon, with Udon, 68, 69
Spicy Meat and Feta Pizza, 134
Steak Asada Tacos with Simple Guacamole, 126
Beets and Kirby Cucumbers, Dilled, 39
Berry(ies)
-Plum Pie Filling, 182
Blueberry Pie Filling, 183
Coriander Lamb Racks with Blackberry Sauce, 136, 137
and Melon Carpaccio with Honey-Mint Syrup, 188
Quick Simple Icebox Cheesecake, 179
Strawberries and Cream with Vanilla Creamcakes, 191
Vanilla Custard Cremes with Blackberries, 192, 193
Black Bean Salad, Warm, Cumin Chicken with, 43
Black Beans, Spicy, 83
Blackberries, Vanilla Custard Cremes with, 192, 193
Blackberry Sauce, Coriander Lamb Racks with, 136, 137
Blueberry Pie Filling, 183
Bok Choy
Miso Soup with Udon, Shiitakes, and, 104, 105
Singapore Noodles, 91
Bread, White Corn Pudding, 46
Broccoli
and Orange Beef Stir-Fry, 135
White Bean–Escarole Soup with Polenta Croutons, 108, 109
Broccoli Raab Bruschetta, 49, 49
Brown Sugar–Yogurt Cakes, 175
Bruschetta, Broccoli Raab, 49, 49
Bulgur Risotto, Lemon-Chard, 90
Burgers, Turkey, Real Good, 139
Butter, Feta, 38

Butter Cake, Simple, 172, *173*
Butternut Squash–Apple Soup, 102

C

Cabbage
    Carrot, and Chickpea Salad, 28, *29*
    Chinese Chicken Noodle Soup, 106
    Miso Soup with Udon, Shiitakes, and Bok Choy, *104,* 105
    Noodles, Panfried, 67
    Root Vegetable Soup, 100, *100*
    Singapore Noodles, 91
Caesar, Easy, 20, *21*
Caesar Dressing, 19
Cake(s)
    Brown Sugar–Yogurt, 175
    Chocolate Birthday, 176, *177*
    Chocolate Pudding, 170
    Simple Butter, 172, *173*
    Spicy Double-Ginger Gingerbread, 174
    Upside-Down Pineapple-Cornmeal, 180
    Vanilla Creamcakes, 190
Cardamom and Ginger–Scented Jasmine Rice, 88, *89*
Carrot, Cabbage, and Chickpea Salad, 28, *29*
Cauliflower, Garlic-Roasted, Ziti with, 71
Cellophane Noodles with Shiitake Mushrooms, 75
Ceviche, Shrimp and Scallop, 154
Chard
    -Lemon Bulgur Risotto, 90
    Stir-Fried Greens and Basil, 55
Cheese
    Baby Spinach with Apples and Goat Feta, 34
    Eggplant Stacks, 52, *53*
    Farfalle with Zucchini and Lemon-Cream Sauce, *72,* 73
    Feta Butter, 38
    Giant Ravioli with Lamb Ragù, 80, *81*
    Grilled Mexican Corn, 58, *58*
    Mac and, with Sage Crumbs, 74
    Quick Simple Icebox Cheesecake, 179
    Spicy Meat and Feta Pizza, 134
    Winter Greens, Grapes, and Gorgonzola Salad, 42
Cheesecake, Quick Simple Icebox, 179
Chicken
    Cumin, with Warm Black Bean Salad, 43
    Herbed Grilled, 142
    with Lemon–Green Olive Sauce, 143
    Noodle Soup, Chinese, 106
    Noodle Soup, Classic, 95
    Poached, Avocado, and Citrus Salad, 23
    Roast, –Chutney Salad, 39
    Salt-and-Pepper Roast Cardamom, *146,* 147
    Satay, Ginger, with Grilled Mango, *144,* 144–45
    Stock, Simple, 94
    Sweet Potato, and Hominy Soup (*Sancocho*), 112, *113*
    Tuscan Peppered Wings, 138
Chickpea, Cabbage, and Carrot Salad, 28, *29*
Chickpeas and Lima Beans with Warm Bacon Dressing, 36, *37*
Chili, Vegetarian, with Grilled Polenta, 110
Chilies
    Curried Monkfish with Tomatoes and, 150
    Steak Asada Tacos with Simple Guacamole, 126
    Sweet Potato–Chipotle Pancakes, 62
Chinese Chicken Noodle Soup, 106
Chipotle–Sweet Potato Pancakes, 62
Chocolate
    -Banana and Pecan Tarts, 186
    Birthday Cake, 176, *177*
    Cowboy Cookies, 169
    Hot, Sorbet, 166
    Pudding Cakes, 170
    –Sour Cream Frosting, 178
    Thin Mints, 171
    Truffle Sauce, 167
Chutney, Fresh Plum, 131
Coconut
    Basmati Rice, 78
    Broth, Thai Curried Mussels in, 162
    Green Thai Vegetable Curry, 51
    Satay Sauce, 145
Cookie Crust, 178
cookie dough, making ahead, 169
Cookies, Cowboy, 169
cooking strategies and tips
    basic kitchen tools, 8, 10
    basic pantry items, 13–14
    basic pots and pans, 8–10
    grocery shopping, 10–11
    organizing kitchen, 7
    organizing pantry, 7–8
    preparing recipes ahead, 7
Coriander Lamb Racks with Blackberry Sauce, 136, *137*
Corn
    Cumin Chicken with Warm Black Bean Salad, 43
    Grilled Mexican, 58, *58*
    Roasted, and Barley Pilaf, 83
    Salsa, Grilled Tomato-, 56, *57*
    Succotash Sauté with Shrimp, 163
    White, Pudding Bread, 46

Couscous Tabbouleh, 87
Cowboy Cookies, 169
Cowboy Steaks with Pico de Gallo, 122
Croutons, Polenta, White Bean–Escarole Soup with, 108, 109
Crust, Cookie, 178
Crust, Sweet Pastry, 185
Cucumber(s)
    -Yogurt Salad with Ginger and Mint, 35
    Couscous Tabbouleh, 87
    Kirby, and Beets, Dilled, 39
    Orecchiette with Spring Peas and Brown Butter, 84, 85
    Parsley Salad on Flatbread with Feta Butter, 38
    Relish, Pickled, 148, 149
Cumin Chicken with Warm Black Bean Salad, 43
Curried Egg Salad with Olives and Capers, 28
Curried Eggplant Omelet with Dill and Tomatoes, 54
Curried Monkfish with Tomatoes and Chilies, 150
Curried Mussels, Thai, in Coconut Broth, 162
Curried Okra and Tomatoes, 47
Curried Tomatoes and Tofu, 101
Curry, Green Thai Vegetable, 51
Curry, Vegetable and Shrimp, 51
Custard Cremes, Vanilla, with Blackberries, 192, 193

D

Desserts
    Baked Candied Apples, 187
    Banana-Chocolate and Pecan Tarts, 186
    Brown Sugar–Yogurt Cakes, 175
    Chocolate Birthday Cake, 176, 177
    Chocolate Pudding Cakes, 170
    Chocolate Thin Mints, 171
    Chocolate Truffle Sauce, 167
    Cowboy Cookies, 169
    Free-Form Fruit Pies, 181, 181–83
    Grilled Banana Splits, 167
    Hot Chocolate Sorbet, 166
    Lemon-Lime Tart, 184
    Melon and Berry Carpaccio with Honey-Mint Syrup, 188
    Quick Simple Icebox Cheesecake, 179
    Simple Butter Cake, 172, 173
    Spicy Double-Ginger Gingerbread, 174
    Strawberries and Cream with Vanilla Creamcakes, 191
    Summer Fruit in Glasses of May Wine, 189, 189
    Upside-Down Pineapple-Cornmeal Cake, 180
    Vanilla Creamcakes, 190

Vanilla Custard Cremes with Blackberries, 192, 193
Dilled Beets and Kirby Cucumbers, 39
Dressings
    Balsamic-Shallot Vinaigrette, 42
    Basic Vinaigrette, 18
    Caesar Dressing, 19
    Miso Vinaigrette, 19
    Quick Vinaigrette, 18

E

Edamame-Quinoa Pilaf, 86
Eggplant
    Green Thai Vegetable Curry, 51
    Omelet, Curried, with Dill and Tomatoes, 54
    Ratatouille, 50
    Roasted, Spread, 57
    Stacks, 52, 53
    Vegetable and Shrimp Curry, 51
Egg(s)
    Asparagus with Prosciutto-Bacon and, 48, 48
    Curried Eggplant Omelet with Dill and Tomatoes, 54
    Penne, Ham, and Asparagus Frittata, 76, 77
    Salad, Curried, with Olives and Capers, 28
    Salad, Tuscan, 24, 25
    Turkish Meat Loaf, 140, 141
    Vegetable Fried Brown Rice, 79
Escarole–White Bean Soup with Polenta Croutons, 108, 109

F

Farfalle with Zucchini and Lemon-Cream Sauce, 72, 73
Fennel
    Parsnip-Potato Soup, 95
    Root Vegetable Soup, 100, 100
    Simple Fish Stew, 119
    Spring Chopped Salad with Lime-Mint Vinaigrette, 32, 33
    Winter Greens, Grapes, and Gorgonzola Salad, 42
Feta, Goat, Baby Spinach with Apples and, 34
Feta and Meat Pizza, Spicy, 134
Feta Butter, 38
Fish. *See also* Shellfish
    Barbecued Salmon with Potatoes, 159
    Curried Monkfish with Tomatoes and Chilies, 150
    Panko-Crusted, and Chips, 151
    Roasted Whole Snapper on a Bed of Lemons, 156, 157
    Sake-Marinated Tuna Steaks with Miso Vinaigrette, 155
    Smoked Salmon and Avocado Salad, 35

Sole with Tomato-Butter Sauce, 158
Stew, Simple, 119
Swordfish Masala Kebabs with Mango Raita, 152, 153
Teriyaki-Glazed Salmon with Pickled Cucumber Relish, 148, 149
Tuna Steak Salad with Olive Vinaigrette, 22
Warm Pasta Salad with Tuna-Tomato Sauce, 31
Flatbread, Parsley Salad on, with Feta Butter, 38
French Onion Soup, 103
Frittata, Penne, Ham, and Asparagus, 76, 77
Frosting, Chocolate–Sour Cream, 178
Fruit. See also Berry(ies); specific fruits
Asian Spiced, 27
Pies, Free-Form, 181, 181–83
Quick Simple Icebox Cheesecake, 179
Summer, in Glasses of May Wine, 189, 189

G

Garlic Mashed Potatoes with Peas, 59
Garlic-Roasted Cauliflower, Ziti with, 71
Ginger and Cardamom–Scented Jasmine Rice, 88, 89
Ginger and Mint, Cucumber-Yogurt Salad with, 35
Ginger Chicken Satay with Grilled Mango, 144, 144–45
Gingerbread, Spicy Double-Ginger, 174
Goat Feta, Baby Spinach with Apples and, 34
Gorgonzola, Winter Greens, and Grapes Salad, 42
Grapes, Winter Greens, and Gorgonzola Salad, 42
Green Thai Vegetable Curry, 51
Greens. See also Cabbage
Baby Spinach with Apples and Goat Feta, 34
and Basil, Stir-Fried, 55
Easy Caesar, 20, 21
Lemon-Chard Bulgur Risotto, 90
Linguine with Walnuts and Arugula, 70
Recipe for a Simple Salad, 20, 20
Singapore Noodles, 91
Spicy Cinnamon Beef with Udon, 68, 69
Spring Chopped Salad with Lime-Mint Vinaigrette, 32, 33
Tuscan Egg Salad, 24, 25
washing and storing, 17
White Bean–Escarole Soup with Polenta Croutons, 108, 109
Winter, Grapes, and Gorgonzola Salad, 42
Guacamole, Simple, 126

H

Ham
Penne, and Asparagus Frittata, 76, 77

Singapore Noodles, 91
Herbed Grilled Chicken, 142
Hominy, Chicken, and Sweet Potato Soup (Sancocho), 112, 113
Honey-Grilled Pork Tenderloin with Fresh Plum Chutney, 131
Hot and Sour Shrimp Soup, 96, 97

J

Jasmine Rice, Ginger and Cardamom–Scented, 88, 89
Juniper-Steamed Lobster with Ginger Butter, 160

K

Kebabs
Ginger Chicken Satay with Grilled Mango, 144, 144–45
Skewered Shrimp with Duck Sauce, 163
Swordfish Masala, with Mango Raita, 152, 153
kitchen tools, 8, 10
knives, 10

L

Lamb
Racks, Coriander, with Blackberry Sauce, 136, 137
Ragù, 82
Ragù, Giant Ravioli with, 80, 81
Spicy Meat and Feta Pizza, 134
Tagine, 114
Turkish Meat Loaf, 140, 141
Lemon-Chard Bulgur Risotto, 90
Lemon-Cream Sauce, Farfalle with Zucchini and, 72, 73
Lemon-Lime Tart, 184
lemongrass, buying, 96
Lemons, Roasted Whole Snapper on a Bed of, 156, 157
Lentil-Rice Soup, 107
Lentils, Stewed, with Chorizo and Queso Fresco, 116, 117
Lentils and Fried Onions, Salt-Baked Crushed Potatoes with, 60, 61
Lima Beans and Chickpeas with Warm Bacon Dressing, 36, 37
Linguine with Walnuts and Arugula, 70
Lobster, Juniper-Steamed, with Ginger Butter, 160

M

Mac and Cheese with Sage Crumbs, 74
Mango(es)
Asian Spiced Fruit, 27
Grilled, Ginger Chicken Satay with, 144, 144–45
Raita, Swordfish Masala Kebabs with, 152, 153

Meat. *See* Beef; Lamb; Pork; Veal

Meat Loaf, Turkish, 140, *141*

Melon and Berry Carpaccio with Honey-Mint Syrup, 188

miso, buying, 105

Miso Soup with Udon, Shiitakes, and Bok Choy, *104, 105*

Miso Vinaigrette, 19

Monkfish, Curried, with Tomatoes and Chilies, 150

Mushrooms

    Hot and Sour Shrimp Soup, 96, *97*

    Miso Soup with Udon, Shiitakes, and Bok Choy, *104,*
        105

    Shiitake, Cellophane Noodles with, 75

Mussels

    Quick Simple Paella, 161

    Thai Curried, in Coconut Broth, 162

N

Noodle(s)

    Cellophane, with Shiitake Mushrooms, 75

    Hot and Sour Shrimp Soup, 96, *97*

    Miso Soup with Udon, Shiitakes, and Bok Choy, *104,*
        105

    Orange Beef and Broccoli Stir-Fry, 135

    Panfried Cabbage, 67

    Singapore, 91

    Soba, Cold, 41, *41*

    Soup, Chicken, Chinese, 106

    Soup, Chicken, Classic, 95

    Spicy Cinnamon Beef with Udon, 68, *69*

O

Okra and Tomatoes, Curried, 47

Olive(s)

    and Capers, Curried Egg Salad with, 28

    and Dill, Warm Potato Salad with, 26

    Green, –Lemon Sauce, Chicken with, 143

    Green, Tapenade, 123

    Vinaigrette, Tuna Steak Salad with, 22

Omelet, Curried Eggplant, with Dill and Tomatoes, 54

Onion Soup, French, 103

onions, grating, 139

Orange(s)

    Beef and Broccoli Stir-Fry, 135

    Poached Chicken, Avocado, and Citrus Salad, 23

    rinds, grating, 135

Orecchiette with Spring Peas and Brown Butter, 84, *85*

P

Paella, Quick Simple, 161

Pancakes, Sweet Potato–Chipotle, 62

Panko-Crusted Fish and Chips, 151

pantry items, basic, 13–14

pantry items, organizing, 7–8

Parsley

    Couscous Tabbouleh, 87

    Salad on Flatbread with Feta Butter, 38

Parsnip-Potato Soup, 95

Pasta. *See also* Noodle(s)

    Farfalle with Zucchini and Lemon-Cream Sauce, *72,*
        73

    Giant Ravioli with Lamb Ragù, 80, *81*

    Linguine with Walnuts and Arugula, 70

    Mac and Cheese with Sage Crumbs, 74

    Orecchiette with Spring Peas and Brown Butter, 84,
        85

    Penne, Ham, and Asparagus Frittata, 76, *77*

    Salad, Warm, with Tuna-Tomato Sauce, 31

    Spaghetti with Roast Tomato Sauce, 66

    Ziti with Garlic-Roasted Cauliflower, 71

Pastry Crust, Sweet, 185

Peaches

    Asian Spiced Fruit, 27

    Quick Simple Icebox Cheesecake, 179

Peas

    Garlic Mashed Potatoes with, 59

    Quick Simple Paella, 161

    Spring, and Brown Butter, Orecchiette with, 84, *85*

Pecan(s)

    Baby Spinach with Apples and Goat Feta, 34

    and Banana-Chocolate Tarts, 186

Penne, Ham, and Asparagus Frittata, 76, *77*

Peppers

    Curried Monkfish with Tomatoes and Chilies, 150

    Ratatouille, 50

    Steak Asada Tacos with Simple Guacamole, 126

    Sweet Potato–Chipotle Pancakes, 62

Pesto, Simple, 50

Picadillo, Plantains with, 127

Pickled Cucumber Relish, *148,* 149

Pico de Gallo, 122

Piecrust, Basic, with Four Fillings, 182–83

Pies, Free-Form Fruit, *181,* 181–83

Pilaf, Quinoa-Edamame, 86

Pilaf, Roasted Corn and Barley, 83

Pineapple

    -Cornmeal Cake, Upside-Down, 180

    Asian Spiced Fruit, 27

Pizza, Spicy Meat and Feta, 134

pizza dough, defrosting, 134

Plantains with Picadillo, 127

Plum-Berry Pie Filling, 182

Plum Chutney, Fresh, 131

Polenta, Grilled, Vegetarian Chili with, 110

polenta, precooked, buying, 111

Polenta Croutons, White Bean–Escarole Soup with, 108,
    109

Polenta Rounds, Grilled, 111

Pork

    Asparagus with Prosciutto-Bacon and Eggs, 48, 48

    Lima Beans and Chickpeas with Warm Bacon Dress-
        ing, 36, 37

    Penne, Ham, and Asparagus Frittata, 76, 77

    Plantains with Picadillo, 127

    Quick Simple Paella, 161

    Singapore Noodles, 91

    Stewed Lentils with Chorizo and Queso Fresco, 116,
        117

    Tarragon-Crusted Loin Chops, 130

    Tenderloin, Honey-Grilled, with Fresh Plum Chut-
        ney, 131

    Tenderloins, Tamarind-Glazed, 132, 133

    Thai-Style Sausage Salad, 40, 40

    Turkish Meat Loaf, 140, 141

Potato(es)

    -Parsnip Soup, 95

    Barbecued Salmon with, 159

    Mashed, Basil, 59

    Mashed, Garlic, with Peas, 59

    Mashed, Simple, 59

    Mashed, Wasabi, 59

    Oven Frites, 62

    Root Vegetable Soup, 100, 100

    Salad, Warm, with Olives and Dill, 26

    Salt-Baked Crushed, with Lentils and Fried Onions,
        60, 61

    Stewed Lentils with Chorizo and Queso Fresco, 116,
        117

    Sweet, Baked, 63

    Sweet, –Chipotle Pancakes, 62

pots and pans, 8–10

Poultry. See Chicken; Turkey

Prosciutto-Bacon and Eggs, Asparagus with, 48, 48

Q

Quinoa-Edamame Pilaf, 86

R

Radicchio

    Cabbage, Carrot, and Chickpea Salad, 28, 29

    Winter Greens, Grapes, and Gorgonzola Salad, 42

Ratatouille, 50

Ravioli, Giant, with Lamb Ragù, 80, 81

Relish, Pickled Cucumber, 148, 149

Rice

    Brown, Vegetable Fried, 79

    Coconut Basmati, 78

    Jasmine, Ginger and Cardamom–Scented, 88, 89

    Quick Simple Paella, 161

    Yellow Saffron, 78

Risotto, Lemon-Chard Bulgur, 90

Rosemary-Wrapped Filet Mignon, 128, 129

S

Saffron Rice, Yellow, 78

Sake-Marinated Tuna Steaks with Miso Vinaigrette, 155

Salad

    Beets and Kirby Cucumbers, Dilled, 39

    Black Bean, Warm, Cumin Chicken with, 43

    Cabbage, Carrot, and Chickpea, 28, 29

    Couscous Tabbouleh, 87

    Cucumber-Yogurt, with Ginger and Mint, 35

    Easy Caesar, 20, 21

    Egg, Curried, with Olives and Capers, 28

    Egg, Tuscan, 24, 25

    Fruit, Asian Spiced, 27

    Lima Beans and Chickpeas with Warm Bacon Dress-
        ing, 36, 37

    Parsley, on Flatbread with Feta Butter, 38

    Pasta, Warm, with Tuna-Tomato Sauce, 31

    Poached Chicken, Avocado, and Citrus, 23

    Potato, Warm, with Olives and Dill, 26

    Roast Chicken–Chutney, 39

    Sausage, Thai-Style, 40, 40

    Simple, Recipe for a, 20, 20

    Smoked Salmon and Avocado, 35

    Soba Noodles, Cold, 41, 41

    Spinach, Baby, with Apples and Goat Feta, 34

    Spring Chopped, with Lime-Mint Vinaigrette, 32, 33

    Tomato, Heirloom, with Sweet Basil Vinegar, 31

    Tuna Steak, with Olive Vinaigrette, 22

    Winter Greens, Grapes, and Gorgonzola, 42

salad dressings. See Dressings

Salmon

    Barbecued, with Potatoes, 159

    Smoked, and Avocado Salad, 35

    Teriyaki-Glazed, with Pickled Cucumber Relish, 148,
        149

Salsa

    Grilled Tomato-Corn, 56, 57

    Pico de Gallo, 122

Salt-and-Pepper Roast Cardamom Chicken, 146, 147
Salt-Baked Crushed Potatoes with Lentils and Fried
    Onions, 60, 61
Sancocho (Chicken, Sweet Potato, and Hominy Soup),
    112, 113
Satay, Ginger Chicken, with Grilled Mango, 144, 144–45
Satay Sauce, 145
Sauce
    Basic White, 74
    Chocolate Truffle, 167
    Duck, 163
    Grilled Tomato-Corn Salsa, 56, 57
    Lamb Ragù, 82
    Pico de Gallo, 122
    Roast Tomato, 66
    Satay, 145
    Simple Pesto, 50
Sausage(s)
    Quick Simple Paella, 161
    Salad, Thai-Style, 40, 40
    Stewed Lentils with Chorizo and Queso Fresco, 116,
        117
    Turkish Meat Loaf, 140, 141
Scallop and Shrimp Ceviche, 154
Shellfish
    Hot and Sour Shrimp Soup, 96, 97
    Juniper-Steamed Lobster with Ginger Butter, 160
    Quick Simple Paella, 161
    Shrimp and Scallop Ceviche, 154
    Simple Fish Stew, 119
    Singapore Noodles, 91
    Skewered Shrimp with Duck Sauce, 163
    Succotash Sauté with Shrimp, 163
    Thai Curried Mussels in Coconut Broth, 162
    Vegetable and Shrimp Curry, 51
Shiitake Mushrooms, Cellophane Noodles with, 75
Shiitakes, Udon, and Bok Choy, Miso Soup with, 104, 105
Shrimp
    Quick Simple Paella, 161
    and Scallop Ceviche, 154
    Simple Fish Stew, 119
    Singapore Noodles, 91
    Skewered, with Duck Sauce, 163
    Soup, Hot and Sour, 96, 97
    Succotash Sauté with, 163
    and Vegetable Curry, 51
Singapore Noodles, 91
Skewered Shrimp with Duck Sauce, 163
skillets, 9
Smoked Salmon and Avocado Salad, 35

Snapper, Roasted Whole, on a Bed of Lemons, 156, 157
Soba Noodles, Cold, 41, 41
Sole with Tomato-Butter Sauce, 158
Sorbet, Hot Chocolate, 166
Soup. See also Stew
    Butternut Squash–Apple, 102
    Chicken, Sweet Potato, and Hominy (Sancocho), 112,
        113
    Chicken Noodle, Chinese, 106
    Chicken Noodle, Classic, 95
    French Onion, 103
    Lentil-Rice, 107
    Miso, with Udon, Shiitakes, and Bok Choy, 104, 105
    Parsnip-Potato, 95
    Root Vegetable, 100, 100
    Shrimp, Hot and Sour, 96, 97
    Simple Chicken Stock, 94
    Tomato, Cream of, 99
    Tomato, Fresh, 99
    Vegetable Stock, 94
    White Bean–Escarole, with Polenta Croutons, 108, 109
Sour Cream–Chocolate Frosting, 178
Spaghetti with Roast Tomato Sauce, 66
Spinach
    Baby, with Apples and Goat Feta, 34
    Spicy Cinnamon Beef with Udon, 68, 69
    Stir-Fried Greens and Basil, 55
Spreads
    Feta Butter, 38
    Fresh Plum Chutney, 131
    Green Olive Tapenade, 123
    Roasted Eggplant, 57
    Simple Guacamole, 126
Squash
    Butternut, –Apple Soup, 102
    Farfalle with Zucchini and Lemon-Cream Sauce, 72,
        73
    Ratatouille, 50
    Root Vegetable Soup, 100, 100
Stew
    Curried Tomatoes and Tofu, 101
    Fish, Simple, 119
    Lamb Tagine, 114
    Stewed Lentils with Chorizo and Queso Fresco, 116,
        117
    Vegetarian Chili with Grilled Polenta, 110
Stock, Simple Chicken, 94
Stock, Vegetable, 94
Strawberries and Cream with Vanilla Creamcakes, 191
Succotash Sauté with Shrimp, 163

Sweet Potato–Chipotle Pancakes, 62
Sweet Potatoes, Baked, 63
Swordfish Masala Kebabs with Mango Raita, 152, 153

T

Tabbouleh, Couscous, 87
Tacos, Steak Asada, with Simple Guacamole, 126
Tamarind-Glazed Pork Tenderloins, 132, 133
Tapenade, Green Olive, 123
Tarragon-Crusted Loin Chops, 130
Tart, Lemon-Lime, 184
Tarts, Banana-Chocolate and Pecan, 186
Teriyaki-Glazed Salmon with Pickled Cucumber Relish,
        148, 149
Thai Curried Mussels in Coconut Broth, 162
Thai-Style Sausage Salad, 40, 40
Thin Mints, Chocolate, 171
Tofu, Curried Tomatoes and, 101
Tomato(es)
        -Butter Sauce, Sole with, 158
        -Tuna Sauce, Warm Pasta Salad with, 31
        and Chilies, Curried Monkfish with, 150
        Curried Eggplant Omelet with Dill and, 54
        Curried Okra and, 47
        Eggplant Stacks, 52, 53
        Heirloom, Salad with Sweet Basil Vinegar, 31
        Lamb Ragù, 82
        Pico de Gallo, 122
        Plantains with Picadillo, 127
        Roast, Sauce, Spaghetti with, 66
        Salsa, Grilled Corn-, 56, 57
        Simple Fish Stew, 119
        Soup, Cream of, 99
        Soup, Fresh, 99
        and Tofu, Curried, 101
Tuna
        -Tomato Sauce, Warm Pasta Salad with, 31
        Steak Salad with Olive Vinaigrette, 22
        Steaks, Sake-Marinated, with Miso Vinaigrette, 155
Turkey
        Burgers, Real Good, 139
        Turkish Meat Loaf, 140, 141
Turkish Meat Loaf, 140, 141
Tuscan Egg Salad, 24, 25
Tuscan Peppered Wings, 138

U

Udon, Shiitakes, and Bok Choy, Miso Soup with, 104, 105
Udon, Spicy Cinnamon Beef with, 68, 69
Upside-Down Pineapple-Cornmeal Cake, 180

V

Vanilla Creamcakes, 190
Vanilla Custard Cremes with Blackberries, 192, 193
Veal
        Tarragon-Crusted Loin Chops, 130
        Turkish Meat Loaf, 140, 141
Vegetable(s), 46–63. See also specific vegetables
        Curry, Green Thai, 51
        Fried Brown Rice, 79
        Root, Soup, 100, 100
        and Shrimp Curry, 51
        Stock, 94
Vegetarian Chili with Grilled Polenta, 110
Vinaigrette, Balsamic-Shallot, 42
Vinaigrette, Basic, 18
Vinaigrette, Miso, 19
Vinaigrette, Quick, 18

W

Walnuts
        and Arugula, Linguine with, 70
        Winter Greens, Grapes, and Gorgonzola Salad, 42
Wasabi Mashed Potatoes, 59
White Bean–Escarole Soup with Polenta Croutons, 108,
        109
White Corn Pudding Bread, 46

Y

Yellow Saffron Rice, 78
Yogurt-Cucumber Salad with Ginger and Mint, 35

Z

Ziti with Garlic-Roasted Cauliflower, 71
Zucchini
        and Lemon-Cream Sauce, Farfalle with, 72, 73
        Ratatouille, 50